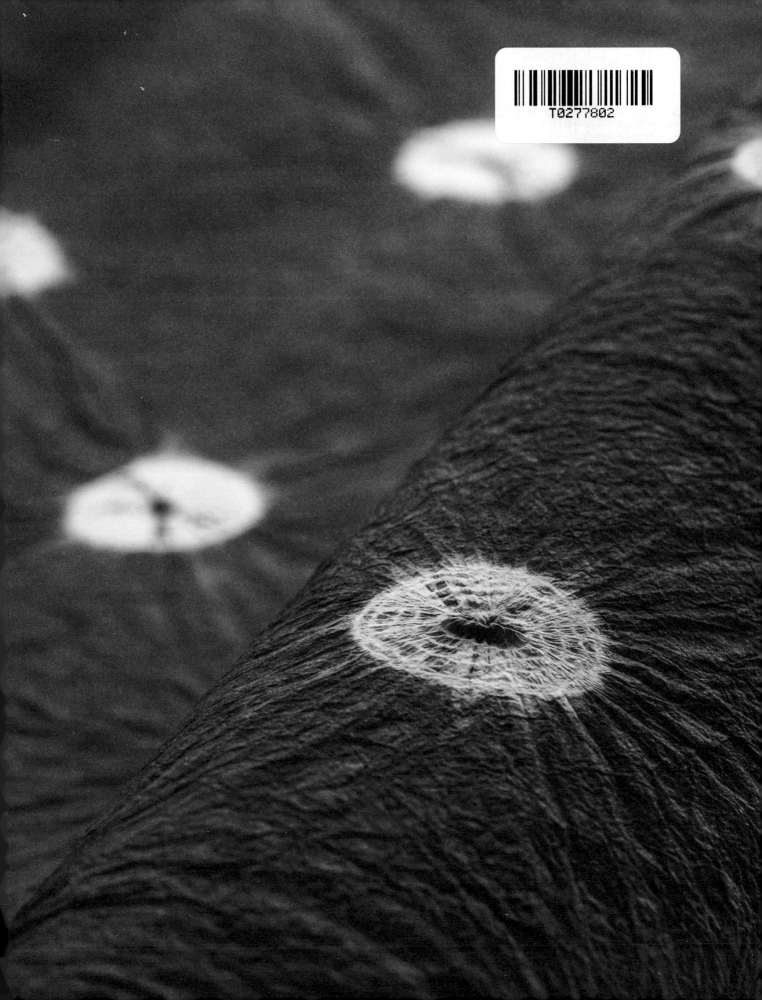

Art, Craft & Community

BOOKS

Edited by
London Centre for Book Arts

Words by
Antonia Williams

Essays by
Kathy Abbott, Tom Frith-Powell,
Megan N. Liberty & Brooke Palmieri

Ludion

Introduction p. 6
Ira Yonemura and Simon Goode

Artists' Books as Community p. 14
Megan N. Liberty

An Introduction to Printing p. 42
Brooke Palmieri

An Introduction to Bookbinding p. 124
Kathy Abbott

An Introduction to Papermaking p. 166
Tom Frith-Powell

Reading List p. 218

Art

Craft

Community

Laurel Parker Book p. 22
Outer Space Press p. 30
The Brother in Elysium p. 36
Éditions du Livre p. 52
Three Star Books p. 58
Candor Arts p. 64
Book Works p. 70
Sheryl Oppenheim p. 76
Inka Bell p. 84

Kathy Abbott p. 92
Kate Brett p. 98
Kamisoe p. 106
Esme Winter p. 112
Émilie Fayet p. 118
El Lanham p. 130
Morina Mongin p. 138
Awagami Factory p. 148
Tracey Rowledge p. 154
James Cropper Mill
& The Paper Foundation p. 160

Rabbits Road Press p. 176
Tenderbooks p. 182
Utrecht p. 188
Granby Press p. 194
Colorama p. 200
Asami Murakami p. 206
Book/Shop p. 212

London Centre for Book Arts

J. WENZEL

J. WENZEL'S NEEDLES & THREAD
15 METRES
J. WENZEL

Introduction

Ira Yonemura and Simon Goode
London Centre for Book Arts

When we were approached to put together a 'book about books', we jumped at the opportunity. Here was a chance to celebrate people whose work by its very nature takes place behind the scenes, in studios tucked away from view, and whose credit – if they are credited at all – you would find hidden away in the fine print.

At the most basic level, a book is typically made up of a front and back cover, pages and a spine. For such a recognisable object of unquestionable historical and cultural significance, the book has experienced a seemingly never-ending identity crisis since the beginning of the twentieth century, led largely by changes in the way that books are commonly bought and sold, with the introduction of mass-market paperbacks, e-books and other competing technologies. After decades of facing challenges and questions about their very existence, books – and the people and communities who make them – should best be thought of as heterogenous and democratic, as a constellation of many voices and many approaches. Book making, like most of life, is a mess, and one that we find endlessly inspiring.

The process of how simple materials are transformed into the recognisable form of a book can take infinite different routes

and often involves a number of highly skilled artists, technicians and craftspeople such as papermakers, printers, marblers, bookbinders, finishers and gilders. Although it can be a relatively simple and affordable process, certain processes can require machines and equipment that are hard to find and prohibitively expensive for the individual. The London Centre for Book Arts (LCBA) came out of our own personal needs as artists, as well as what we saw as a collective need in London for a genuinely affordable way for people to access facilities for printing, binding and publishing books. We realised that the economic and political realities of being an artist (particularly in a city like London) meant that it would be nearly impossible to do this on your own. We came to the conclusion that sharing, or working together, is the only real model for creating and establishing a fair, dignified and sustainable way of working. It took years to collect the few machines we had, but when we finally opened our doors to the public in 2012 we had just enough for a functioning bindery and print studio.

The LCBA is located in the east London neighbourhood known as Fish Island – just across the road from the Queen Elizabeth Olympic Park, the setting of the 2012 Olympic Games – in what was once the heart of the capital's print industry. The building that currently houses LCBA was once home to a commercial printer

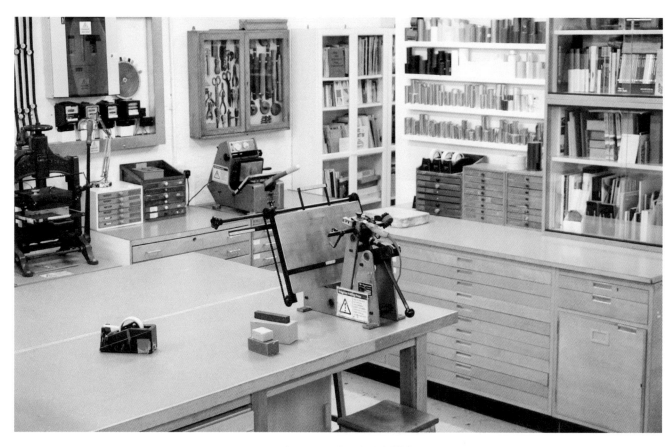

Make Books Not Bombs by Abbie Freeman (Snootie Studios), 2019.

and lithographer. As technologies change, so has the industry, and in recent times the community of Fish Island and neighbouring Hackney Wick has grown to become home to one of the highest concentrations of artist studios in Europe.

LCBA operates as an education centre and an open-access studio, which means that people can learn different skills and join as members to have access to a shared working space and all of the specialist equipment and machines that we maintain. The core of our education programme is craft-based, such as bookbinding (books, boxes, portfolios, etc.), printing (letterpress, Risograph, Linocut, etc.), foil blocking and paper marbling. We also run workshops more broadly on publishing, covering the conception, production and distribution of self-published books. Our studio members make up a small but tight-knit community of artists, designers, craftspeople, illustrators, writers, educators, self-publishers, hobbyists and everyone in between – often sharing ideas, expertise, meals and even gardening tips.

The open-access studios at LCBA are divided roughly into four parts: the bindery, print studio, reprographics studio and the reference library.

The bindery consists of nipping presses, a board chopper, an electric guillotine, foil-blocking presses, wooden finishing and laying presses, and all of the hand-tools required to bind books in the traditional (and not-so-traditional) way. We have four foil-blocking presses, commonly used for applying titles to book covers and spines, but also for blocking onto paper and board in metallic and coloured foils. These machines are also used to emboss and deboss paper and card.

In the print studio, you will find a number of flatbed letterpress proof presses, the largest of which can print a sheet up to 25 inches (63.5 cm) wide, and racks of type cabinets full of both wood and metal type in a range of sizes from 6 point to 60 pica. As well as type, we have the means to print from magnesium or polymer plates using digital artwork.

The reprographics studio consists of machines that you might not typically find in a traditional bindery or print studio: two Risograph duplicators with fourteen colour drums, a colour laser printer, a perfect binder (for paperback books), coil and wire binders, a paper drill and heavy-duty electric stapler for binding pamphlets.

The studio also houses a comprehensive reference library of books about books, bookbinding, printing, design, typography and related fields, along with artists' books. All of which are accessible to our studio users.

From the start, we took a pragmatic and perhaps a somewhat anti-institutional approach to running the studio: keeping things small, staying independent, and prioritising community and friendships. The personality of the studio, if we can call it that, comes from the marriage of our backgrounds and interests. Simon (born in Wolverhampton, UK) studied Book Arts and Crafts at the London College of Communication (LCC) and was lucky enough to have been taught by the last of the trade bookbinders, printers and print finishers on a course that emphasised a practical and craft-based approach to 'book arts'. Ira (born in Kagoshima, Japan), meanwhile, studied Painting and Drawing at the School of the Art Institute of Chicago and around the same time fell into a community of artists, musicians and queer activists who saw books and publishing as an extension of their practices and self-organisation, and collaboration as their de facto model of working.

There are a number of well-established book art centres in the US, with the Center for Book Arts in New York being the oldest, established in 1979. At the beginning, we loosely modelled our studio on similar book centres in the US, particularly the Center for Book Arts, the Minnesota Center for Book Arts and the San

Francisco Center for the Book. All of these organisations have a similar mission and origin story: they began as a way for a group of artists to work, teach, exhibit and find mainstream acceptance for 'book arts', a relatively new concept at the time (see the contribution by Megan N. Liberty on p. 14).

We also took spiritual, if not practical, inspiration from other artist-run studios, galleries and bookshops in the UK and further afield, including Good Press (Glasgow), X Marks the Bökship (London), Golden Age (Chicago), No Coast (Chicago), The Arm (Brooklyn), Eastside Projects (Birmingham, UK), Grand Union (Birmingham, UK), Ooga Booga (Los Angeles), Utrecht (Tokyo, profiled on p. 188) and Printed Matter (New York City) – among many others, who played it a bit loose with their mission and structure to make room for the unexpected.

In the spirit of playing it loose, you may find the selection of profiles in this book a little unorthodox. We wanted to think of the book as a conversation starter, or a way to restart the conversation about books anew. And, like all great conversations, it represents a moment in time, with chance encounters and missed opportunities. After decades of introspection and doubts about its future, the book continues to be an object made with great care and a sense of purpose. Rather than speaking with an injured tone about contemporary book culture, we chose an approach that mimicked the practical, conversational and day-to-day interactions that our studio is built on. In doing so we imagined a kindred community where art and craft, tradition and the contemporary, analogue and digital, and amateur and professional need not be rivals but part of a fertile ecosystem constantly in flux and stronger for it.

Neither Strivers Nor Skivers,
They Will Not Define Us
by Olivia Plender being printed
on a letterpress proofing press
at LCBA in 2020.

Artists' Books as Community

Megan N. Liberty

Artists' books make use of the inherent characteristics of the book form, such as sequence, repetition and tactility. They are durational like film, require participation like performance, and have multidimensional properties like sculpture. And, of course, they can be read like literature and viewed like visual art. The legacy of this field is often traced to the early 1970s, when writers, artists, publishers and galleries began to gather these objects under the umbrella of artists' books.[1] In 1973 Diane Perry Vanderlip curated an exhibition entitled 'Artists Books' at Moore College in Philadelphia, marking the first use of this term in an exhibition of books made by artists. As artist and critic John Perreault wrote in his essay for the catalogue, 'Books as art are not books about art or books of reproductions of art or books of visual material illustrating literary texts, but are books that make art statements in their own right, within the context of art rather than of literature.'[2] Since then, librarians, artists, writers and researchers have continued to debate an exact definition (and consistent term) for these multidisciplinary books as artwork.

The efforts to define artists' books most famously include those of artist and publisher Ulises Carrión, art librarian Clive Phillpot, artist and scholar Lucy Lippard, artist and information studies scholar Johanna Drucker, and former director of the Minnesota Center for Books Arts, Betty Bright.[3] Phillpot, who tended to prefer the terms 'book art' and 'bookwork' for their emphasis on the

fig. 1
Cover of *Art Documen-
tation: Bulletin of the
Art Libraries Society of
North America* 1, no. 6
(Dec 1982).

fig. 2
Michael Snow, *Cover to
Cover*. Halifax: Press of
the Nova Scotia College
of Art and Design, 1975.

object rather than maker, in his own writings defined bookwork
(a term coined by Ulises Carrión in 1978) as '[a]rtwork dependent
upon the structure of a book'.[4] Consider the photobook *Cover to
Cover* (Nova Scotia College of Art and Design, 1975), by filmmaker
and photographer Michael Snow. This book of offset-printed,
full-bleed, black-and-white photographs can be read from front
to back or back to front.[5] The front and back covers show a door
cropped to the edge of the book, with the back cover revealing
fingers grabbing the top right corner. As we flip through the pages,
we move through the doorway and the space, where at times
mirrors and reflections show Snow himself behind the camera.
The book takes us through a physical space, but it requires the
turning of the page as an opening of the door, linking the physical
space of the book to the physical spaces shown.

Artists' books unite the conceptual idea of a book with the craft of
a book, considering how the specific materials make it work. As
the books and publishing practices represented in this collection
attest, there is no singular medium for book art – artists' books
make use of fast and cheap publishing materials, such as photo-
copiers and staples, as well as more expensive and at times deli-
cate materials such as handmade paper and hand-sewn binding.
Artists' books can be published by a trade publisher, a small press,
a collective, or self-published; and the image-making can be done
through photography, printmaking, drawing, typing and even
collage. For the work to be a successful artists' book, it must
consider how these processes translate to book form, and make
use of the qualities of the book.

fig. 1

fig. 2

Madeline Gins's *WORD RAIN* (Grossman Publishers, 1969), an extremely meta and self-referential book, connects the reader's physical experience to the structure of the physical book.[6] Unlike Snow's book, *WORD RAIN* is primarily text, save a few photographic interventions that place fingers on the edges of pages, much like the hand on the edge of *Cover to Cover*. The narrative is one of reading, as we follow the heroine attempting to finish reading a manuscript, while continuously getting bored and distracted. As the narrator's focus drifts, words are left out of the text, forcing us to skim as she does. 'I skimmed over the conversation as it flowed on over the page,' Gins writes. The fingers along edges of the pages mimic our own fingers grasping at the book as we read.[7] While *WORD RAIN* is strikingly visually different from *Cover to Cover*, both books are carefully crafted to generate attention to the turning page and the mental and physical movement of the reader through the book.

Another example, equally dependent on turning pages, draws on the other side of craft, self-published hand-sewn books. In 1972 Keith Smith, who came to making books by way of photography, textiles and printmaking, produced the unique book *Stitches* (Book 28) (keith smith *BOOKS*), the first of his 'No-Picture Books' composed of blank sheets with holes, using light to cast shadows across the pages. *Stitches* is also the first of these books to use string threaded through the holes in the pages. As he writes about a later string book, Book 91 (1982), 'This book deals with cast light and shadows. The light spots are caused by viewing the book with a single light source at 45° angle and three feet to the left of the book.'[8] These specific instructions for lighting the book create

fig. 3
Madeline Gins,
cover and title page
of *WORD RAIN*.
New York: Grossman
Publishers, 1969.

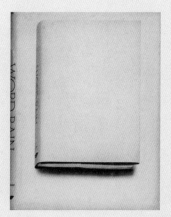
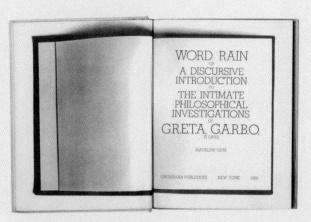

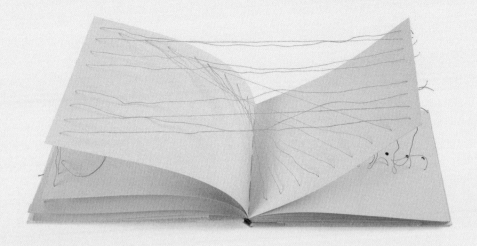

the shadows that become the visual content, making the reading experience also a performative event. While this work is not narrative in the same way that *Cover to Cover* or *WORD RAIN* is, it similarly makes meaning out of the coupling of the book's form and our readerly engagement of turning pages.

And then, of course, there are books that take different forms, reshaping them towards sculpture, like Clarissa Sligh's *What's Happening with Momma?* (Women's Studio Workshop, 1988). This letterpress and silkscreen-printed accordion-fold book re-counts Sligh's experience of the birth of her baby sister. Shaped like a house, the space in which the drama of the story occurs, when the book is unfolded, it stands up like a row of houses, the photographs like large windows into the home, with the six pages of text hanging below them, unfurling like stairs to the building. The naivety of the book's form recalls a child's dolls' house, aligning form and content.

Artists' books emerged during a revolutionary moment for art, giving voice to social justice movements like women's rights, gay rights and the AIDS crisis. In the midst of this, artists realised the power of publishing. This ethos of empowerment and social change is felt in much of the early language around artists' books, an anti-capitalist rhetoric that presents artists' books as a way out of a system that does not serve artists or the public. In 1977 Lippard writes of a 'new awareness of how art (especially the costly "precious object") can be used as a commodity by a capitalist society, new extra-art subject matter, and a rebellion against the increasing elitism of the art world and its planned obsolescence'. But, as Lippard herself soon realised and wrote in 1985, this quest for art outside the market ultimately failed. 'There is a certain irony to all this exposure of conspicuous consumption in that artists' books themselves are distinctly luxury items, commodities with dubious exchange value on the current market.'[9] But all hope is not lost.

In the years since the term 'artists' book' emerged, the practice of making books as art has grown into an expanded notion of publishing within the book arts. It is this expansion that allows for the potential radical notion of publishing that began its popularity. Artists' books are just one of many contemporary book art practices, such as publishing and printmaking (Candor Arts, Inka Bell, Jon Beacham's The Brother in Elysium, Three Star Books, and in particular a number of community Risograph studios such as Colorama, Sumuyya Khader's Granby Press and Rabbits Road Press), design and binding (Asami Murakami, El Lanham, Émilie Fayet, Morina Mongin and Tracey Rowledge), and papermaking and marbling (Esme Winter and Sheryl Oppenheim). This spectrum represents a vast and networked community of support – financial, material and communal – for practices that may not otherwise be possible. As Paul Soulellis said in his talk, 'Urgent Publishing after the Artist's Book', publishing is a radical and political act.[10] The craft practices represented here carry this legacy: Candor Arts, in Chicago, offered artists the opportunity to make elegant, beautifully handcrafted books, an expensive opportunity presented cost-free to the artists; with Granby Press, artist Sumuyya Khader builds a community space in a working-class area of Liverpool, making publishing tools and resources available to artists of different racial and economic backgrounds, expanding the community of artist publishers; and Tenderbooks, in London, fosters independent publishing through distribution and publishing. These book art practices are a network, in which artists' books continue to flourish as book as art, books as craft, and books as community. Much as artists' books cannot be contained by discipline, they represent a radical network of book arts practices and publishing communities.

Megan N. Liberty is the art books section editor at the *Brooklyn Rail* and a co-founder of *Book Art Review*, a criticism initiative at Center for Book Arts, New York. Her writing on artists' books, publishing and printmaking has appeared in *Hyperallergic*, *ArtReview*, *Frieze* and elsewhere. She has led and participated in public conversations on artists' books with the *Brooklyn Rail*, Contemporary Artist Book Conference at Printed Matter's Art Book Fair, and Hill Art Foundation, among others. She has an MA in Art History from the Courtauld Institute of Art, London, and a BA in English from Dickinson College, PA.

1 Over the years, these materials have been referred to in a number of ways. I prefer the term 'artist book(s)',but will use the term 'artists' book(s)', to remain consistent with the rest of this volume, but maintain the original terms used in others' writing.

2 John Perreault, 'Some Thoughts on Books as Art,' in *Artists Books: Moore College of Art Gallery* (Philadelphia: Falcon Press, 1973, p. 15).

3 For surveys of these histories and timelines of artists' books, consider: Riva Castleman, *A Century of Artist Books* (New York: Museum of Modern Art, 1994); Stefan Klima, *Artists Books: A Critical Survey of the Literature* (New York: Granary Books, 1998); Johanna Drucker, *The Century of Artists' Books* (New York: Granary Books, 1994; updated in 2004); and Betty Bright, *No Longer Innocent: Book Art in America, 1960–1980* (New York: Granary Books, 2005).

4 Cover, *Art Documentation: Bulletin of the Art Libraries Society of North America* 1, no. 6 (Dec. 1982).

5 Long out of print, this book has recently been made available again in facsimile by Primary Information and Light Industry.

6 Also out of print, this book has been republished in facsimile within the collection, Lucy Ives, ed., *The Saddest Thing is That I Have Had to Use Words: A Madeline Gins Reader* (Castskill, NY: Siglio, 2020).

7 Megan N. Liberty, 'On *The Saddest Thing is That I Have Had to Use Words: A Madeline Gins Reader*', Brooklyn Rail (April 2020), https://brooklynrail. org/2020/04/art_books/The-Saddest-Thing-Is-That-I-Have-Had-to-Use-Words-A-Madeline-Gins-Reader

8 Keith Smith, *200 Books by Keith Smith* (Rochester, NY: keith smith BOOKS), p. 149. Additionally, I previously wrote at length about Smith's books and his use of sequence, folded pages and light: 'The sequence of a book is essential to Smith's adoption of the form. "I had to use books because it would allow me to have flow and movement," he told Bock. "I am not interested in the single pictures, I am interested in the totality of the thing. The individual pages have to give up their independence in order to form a union."' In Megan N. Liberty, 'The Tactile Pull of Keith Smith's Book Art', *Hyperallergic*, 21 June 2018: https://hyperallergic.com/448125/keith-smith-book-art-philadelphia-museum-art/

9 Lucy Lippard, 'Conspicuous Consumption: New Artists' Books,' in Joan Lyons, ed., *Artists' Books: A Critical Anthology and Sourcebook* (Rochester, NY: Visual Studies Workshop Press), pp. 49–58.

10 This lecture was given as part of the Contemporary Artist's Book Conference on 27 February 2021 and is now available as a book: Paul Soulellis, *Urgent Publishing After the Artist's Book: Making Public in Movements Towards Liberation* (New York: Gender-Fail, 2021).

ART

Laurel Parker Book

Laurel Parker (born in New Orleans, USA) grew up in New Orleans, Louisiana, before going on to study Fine Arts in Boston, Massachusetts. She later moved to New York which led her to the Center for Book Arts where she took master classes in bookmaking while also teaching there. Since 2008 she has been based in Paris where she runs her eponymous studio, now in the eastern suburb of Romainville.

Laurel Parker Book designs books, boxes and book objects for artists and publishers, as well as for agencies, luxury brands, institutions and the private sector. The studio produces one-of-a-kind or limited editions and thus operates in a different world from large-scale book production. The work is collaborative, developed through discussion with the client, the graphic designer and the printer, as well as with suppliers and other craftspeople. Each project is carried from conception to manufacture, offering services including object design, graphic design and making in the studio.

Parker works with one colleague, Paul Chamard, who started as her intern in 2011, before becoming her assistant and, in 2018, her associate. They also take on interns from time to time, each of whom stays one or two months.

Parker considers her path to bookmaking an unusual one. 'I started making books in art school in Boston. I was painting and making films and heard about an artists' books class. Eventually, I got into the class and really loved it,' she recalls. After graduating, she kept making books by herself and eventually left her day job to go and work in a traditional hand bindery. 'I didn't last long because I didn't like the environment, but I did learn quite a bit. Then, I just started learning on my own

– from technical manuals and trying things out on my own,' she says. Parker also started teaching what she knew to adults, which led her to the Center for Book Arts in New York. She credits most of what she has learned, however, to her time in Paris and working with clients.

'My practice has always evolved in function to the equipment available to me,' Parker says. Buying her first board shear opened up new possibilities, and the same went for her first press. 'Then [came] learning about CNC [computer numerical control] cutters, die cutting, etc. And now, working with Paul – who is a real MacGyver – we are always learning from each other,' she says.

She is most inspired by paper as a material, preferring papers from Japan. The studio practises many specialised techniques but is best known for its clean design and well-made product which always has something a little playful about it. 'I do firmly believe that you cannot be a craftsperson without doing some design work on a project, even if there is someone else making conceptual decisions. There will always be a need to interpret and transform ideas into something workable in the book form,' Parker says.

Although she tries to remain positive, Parker is becoming more sceptical about the future of hand binding in France. But

Laurel Parker folding Japanese paper with digital prints – plant specimens that become origami – for the edition *Folded to Fit* by artist Yann Sérandour. Paris, 2019.

Hand-built presentation case with shelves containing five archival boxes, custom built to hold *Les Sommeils*, original drawings and writings by Robert Denos, for the collection of the Jacques Doucet Literary Library, Paris, 2017.

she is convinced that artists will always need their services. 'They will always want to make books and boxes. This will be our future, with artists, and with restoration,' she says.

When it comes to new technologies, she believes that, if there is a way to make something faster and more neatly, one should embrace that option. 'But I feel the best work uses both handwork *and* new technologies. There are some things that you just cannot do with a machine. But, of course, there are some things that are better by machine than by hand. The trick is to know how to combine the two,' she says.

Laurel Parker Book has had many proud moments as a studio. Most recently, it made a limited-edition portfolio of palladium prints of Frank Hurley's photographs of Sir Ernest Shackleton's trans-Antarctic expedition in the *Endurance* (published by Salto Ulbeek, 2020).

Parker deeply admires books because there is always the element of storytelling. 'Also, like a film you have the element of time, and also that experience of being alone with the book (like in the dark watching a movie). It's a personal experience,' she explains.

Annual end-of-the-year journal, a gift for clients. Card stock with silkscreen printing and hot stamping. Hand-sewn chain stitch in silver thread. Limited edition of 150 copies, 2016.

Deluxe edition of *Shackleton's Endurance: The Photographs of Frank Hurley, 1914–1917.* Archival quality box with removable portfolio tray to hold 68 platinum-palladium prints, 2 booklets and 1 platinum-palladium book. Published by Salto Ulbeek, Royal Geographical Society (with IBG) and the Scott Polar Research Institute.

Inside Outside #2,
by duo Laurel Parker and
Paul Chamard. Japanese
papers, gold thread, wood.
Installation following their
residency at the Villa
Kujoyama in Kyoto, Japan.
Exhibition ¡ *Viva Villa* ! at
the Collection Lambert,
Avignon, 2020.

Like a film you have the element
of time, and also that experience
of being alone with the book.
It's a personal experience.

Left: Paul Chamard making the book *Flor,* by Mateo López. Boards handmade out of Colorplan paper, die-cut into a 1/4 shape, and glued onto buckram cloth, which is then hand-cut along the edges of the boards. Paris, 2019.

Below: Apprentice Sarah Mohisen making the composite boards for *ISO's,* a woven poster. Weaver's cotton cord cut to precise lengths is hand-glued into notches in layered boards, then covered with Takeo papers. A collaboration with designers Undo-Redo and weavers Atelier 3 for Design Days, Musée des Arts Décoratifs, Paris, 2014.

Outer Space Press

Artists Claudio Pogo (born in Freiburg, Germany) and Magdalena Wysocka (born in Jaworzno, Poland) have been running Outer Space Press since 2016. Based in Berlin, Germany, it is a small independent press that creates handcrafted artists' books in small print runs, often in collaboration with other artists and photographers.

'Our studio was created from a dream of being independent,' say Pogo and Wysocka. Pogo had been running Pogobooks since 2010, and Wysocka started to intern there in 2012 before beginning to work on small book projects of her own. Gradually, the duo decided to join forces. 'We both imagine our work conceptually as an art practice as well as the entire book production in a very similar manner,' they explain. 'Making everything by hand really opens up the possibility of experimentation for us — from using unusual

paper stocks and unconventional formats to combining printing techniques. As two neurotic types who are extremely meticulous about detail, we love having full control over the way each book is created. It gives us a sense of freedom.'

Regarding their mission with Outer Space Press, they love the democratic aspect of artists' books and the fact that they can share their work in the form of a book. Keeping the craft of bookbinding alive is equally as important to them as helping to make it appealing to younger people — showing how this tradition can be reinterpreted in a contemporary way.

'What interests us the most is always the concept behind the work and then its translation into the book form. The bookbinding part comes second; it is simply a necessary skill to create work,' say Pogo and Wysocka. They describe their work as a hybrid of sorts, designing, printing and binding almost all of their titles in-house. Their approach to publishing is slow, and they finish each book by hand. 'We became very aware of how time-consuming this process is, but also how much value it brings for us,' they say of their practice. Outer Space Press publishes only limited editions, from 3 to 200 copies. They treat each project individually and work very closely with artists who have usually been invited to participate in the process.

They specialise in printing photographs using a Risograph. Taking on a few selected projects each year, they print slowly on one of the fastest digital printers in the world. For their *67–P* book – printed on a paper made from stone – they fed the printer paper sheets one by one, entirely by hand.

Their second specialty is binding, sewing all their books on a 1964 Brehmer 9 3/4 sewing machine that is at the heart of their bindery. 'It is quite a rare piece of equipment, but works perfectly for our small editions. Thanks to it, our books open fully and lay perfectly flat. It also gives them durability – we want them to survive years of browsing,' say Pogo and Wysocka.

Their creative process relies heavily on the fact that they work as a duo. 'We both have quite different sets of skills which complement each other,' they agree.

When it comes to the creative process, they find inspiration from other books. Whether they are contemporary titles made by other publishers that they

Claudio working on Slava Mogutin's special edition of *STCK BYZ RMX*.

Magda finishing covers of her book *By choice, not chance—*.

Below: A prototype of a cover.
Top right: *By choice, not chance—* inside spread.
Bottom right: *67–P* by Wysocka and Pogo: a photobook about a comet and the famous Rosetta Mission, printed on paper made out of stone.

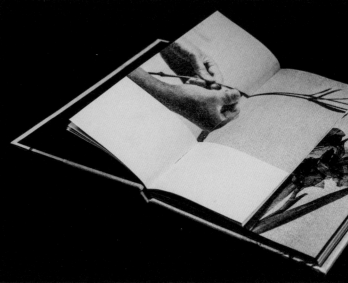

admire, or vintage books that they collect, they are always open to new ideas. From there, they usually build a rough layout, preferring to edit their books the analogue way – using little printouts of the photographs and rearranging them to create a sequence. The next step involves looking closely into materials and choosing the format and edition size, before creating a number of dummies to imagine how the final object might look. 'Every project we have ever created comes with a little collection of these, which we keep as an archive,' they explain. The next step is layout, before they finally start producing the books.

'We love how intimate books are as an art form; the fact that they are objects that invite you to hold them and really have a close connection to them,' say Pogo and Wysocka.

The studio is equipped with a diverse range of bookbinding tools, which are necessary help in the process of making books by hand.

Making everything by hand opens up the possibility of experimentation for us – from using unusual paper stocks and unconventional formats to combining printing techniques.

The Brother
In Elysium

'Personally, I am attracted to limitations, and feel that, in a situation of a limitation, something interesting arises,' says Jon Beacham (born in Cleveland, Ohio) about making everything by hand, which is crucial to his practice. A letterpress printer, publisher and visual artist, he works across various different media, with a heavy focus on printing from metal type.

Beacham grew up in Cleveland, Ohio, but currently lives in Holyoke, Massachusetts, where he works out of his own dedicated studio and runs his press, The Brother In Elysium. His evolution into the multidisciplinary maker he is today started with a one-week basic class in letterpress in the summer of 2007. Initially, he was unclear how exactly he would become involved in printing – he lacked the required tools and did not have access to a studio space. After opening a used bookstore and small exhibition space in Beacon, New York, in

2007, he decided to track down a tabletop press and begin acquiring metal type. Of those early days, he says: 'It's somewhat unclear how I learned typesetting, and my sheer ignorance of how things were actually done helped me. I just thought that you set all the type by hand, and that is how books were made. So I began very early on in with some pretty ambitious projects.' In a stroke of luck, a customer offered him a Vandercook proof press. Ever since then, he has focused on printing books from handset type.

Day to day Beacham works alone, but his Brother In Elysium press arose in the context of collaboration. He explains: 'All of the work I have done with other people arose from deep friendships where collaboration became necessary. Our work, conversations and vision led to projects which both parties feel *had* to be done.'

The role of craft plays an important part in his work, and he finds the process and tools of letterpress printing, specifically typesetting, design and operating a press, very rewarding. He believes this process helps him 'learn by doing', and each book is a process from which he can take new knowledge on to the next book. When he finishes a large project, while feeling satisfied with the job done, Beacham is also immediately aware of what he can do better the next time, leaving space for what is to follow.

Hand-setting texts is an integral part of the books and work he produces, and he has no interest in new technologies, of which he says, 'They don't interest me, and though it may sound severe, I do not wish to pollute myself in becoming acquainted with them.' Instead, he prefers concrete, tangible actions and believes that new technologies, with their endless array of choices, can often lead to uninteresting work.

These books in themselves are akin
to what I feel are portable exhibitions.

He recently felt honoured to work with the Noguchi Museum, New York City, on the publication *I Become a Nisei* – an essay about the artist's self-internment in a prison camp for Japanese Americans during World War II. The essay was originally commissioned by *Reader's Digest*, but remained unpublished. Beacham's first edition was printed from hand-set metal type and was published in association with the museum. This essay was accompanied by images of Noguchi's work relating to that period of his life, chosen from the museum's archive.

Letterpress printing, and book making specifically, has opened up a completely new world for Beacham as a visual artist. 'Starting my publishing imprint The Brother In Elysium has been a vehicle for me to create books that encompass specific bodies of work. These books in themselves are akin to what I feel are portable exhibitions,' he says. Three books which specifically reference this idea are *A Measure of Silence* (2017), *25 East 217th Street* (2018) and *A Symbol of Constancy* (2020).

25 East 217th Street by Jon Beacham.

A Symbol of Constancy: Works on Paper by Jon Beacham. Limited edition with original collage cover.

An Introduction to Printing

Brooke Palmieri

Far from filling a void, the development of printing technology in Europe was instantly, dramatically embedded within a cosmic struggle between angelic conversation and demonic seduction, purity and corruption, heaven and hell. In 1473 the monk and scribe Filippo de Strata wrote to the doge of Venice, Nicolò Marcello, about the growing presence of printers in that city that had begun in 1469:

> This servant of yours has been driven out, bewailing the damage which results from the printers' cunning. They shamelessly print, at a negligible price, material which may, alas, inflame impressionable youths ... Cure (if you will) the plague which is doing away with the laws of all decency, and curb the printers.

> ... Through printing, tender boys and gentle girls, chaste without foul stain, take in whatever mars purity of mind or body; they encourage wantonness, and swallow up huge gain from it ... [Printers] basely flood the market with anything suggestive of sexuality, and they print the stuff at such a low price that anyone and everyone procures it for himself in abundance. And so it happens that asses go to school.

... Writing indeed, which brings in gold for us, should be respected and held to be nobler than all goods, unless she has suffered degradation in the brother of the printing presses. She is a maiden with a pen, a harlot in print. Should you not call her a harlot who makes us excessively amorous? Governed only by avaricious gain, will not the most base woman deserve the name of prostitute, who saps the strength of the young by fostering wantonness? This is what the printing presses do: they corrupt susceptible hearts.[1]

De Strata's intent was for the magistrate to ban printing, since it threatened his career as a scribe – a classic case of turning the personal not only into the political but into a moral panic. On the one hand, his words have the far-fetched quality typical of religious debate at a time when *everything* was a matter of salvation and damnation. Despite the scattering of printing presses in all of the major Italian city-states by this time, books were not widely affordable, nor were literacy rates really equal to his sense of outrage. On the other hand, his language of sexual wantonness, corruption, infectious disease, and hatred for women and sex workers specifically, feels less overblown when read alongside similar reactions at the time, which in turn were drawn from lived experience. Plague *was* a daily reality and a threat, and sex existed on a mind-bending spectrum of divine creativity and demonic ecstasy outside of our contemporary categories and legal codes.[2] And maybe most importantly, printers made good on the panic: de Strata's overblown language was picked up and replicated in many of the texts issued hot off the presses, because sex *sells*, death *sells*. The prefaces and introductory material of many books, pamphlets and broadsides spoke of themselves as objects in exactly these lurid terms, for hundreds of years. And by 1500 there were hundreds of printing presses publishing millions of printed sheets and thousands of books for sale, an incredibly rapid spread of new material that, even if it could not be read by everyone, could at least be perceived by anyone as, indeed, a plague of locusts or a swarm of bees.[3]

Fitting into this cosmology within which printing spread across Europe from the mid-fifteenth century is Matthias Hus's 1499 *La grant Danse Macabre* (The Grand Dance of Death), the earliest known visual depiction of a printing press. All the usual suspects

fig. 1
This woodcut from 1499 is the earliest known visual depiction of a printing press. It is included in the picture book known as the *Danse macabre*, whose verses emphasise that death comes to all, from popes and emperors to ploughmen, was first printed in Paris in 1486. The many Paris editions of *Danse macabre* do not include the printing shop. It is one of three new scenes added to the Lyons version printed by Matthias Hus in 1499. Woodcut from *Grant danse macabre des hommes et des femmes* (f. 7r), 1499.

of book making as they worked together for over three centuries of handpress printing are more or less all accounted for in this depiction. A compositor sits with a composing stick before a case, setting the type; one pressman holds the inking balls, ready to apply ink to the type form already locked into the handpress; another is the muscleman, about to add the paper and pull the lever to impress the ink upon the page. To the far right, a bookseller sits among the finished, bound books – the binder has been left out this time around, as have the distributors. All of these people are being set upon by skeletons – Death personified: a skeleton guiding the arm of the compositor; another skeleton messing up the pressmen's work; yet another grabbing at the bookseller, ready to drag him to whatever afterlife he deserves, which, from the look on his face and his hands raised in a defensive gesture, is not a good one. Working within an iconographic tradition dating back to at least the Middle Ages, *La grant Danse Macabre* thrusts this burgeoning class of new artisans and labourers of the press squarely within the shared reality of popes, emperors, nobles, men and women of all ages and ranks: *No Matter Who You Are, No Matter How Novel your Invention, You Will Die.*

As a colonising force funded and controlled by the government, the university or the missionary abroad, printing was seen as a triumphant technology.[4] But equally it was a source of criticism for these exertions of power and especially – as a means of circulating translations and radical interpretations of the Bible – a dangerous tool of heretics. As for those heretics, they themselves flipped the script and celebrated their use of print to question authority. As John Foxe wrote in his expansive *Book of Martyrs* (1563), a bestselling compendium of religious heretics, mystics and others who had broken with the Roman Catholic Church:

> [H]ereby tongues are known, knowledge groweth, judgment increaseth, books are dispersed, the Scripture is seen, the doctors be read, stories be opened, times compared, truth discerned, falsehood detected, and with finger pointed, and all, as I said, through the benefit of printing. Wherefore, I suppose, that either the pope must abolish printing, or he must seek a new world to reign over; for else, as this world standeth, printing doubtless will abolish him.[5]

The late Elizabeth Eisenstein summarised the perception of moveable type in its first three centuries of use in her final book as both a 'divine art' and an 'infernal machine', depending on into whose hands the technology had fallen. Such a perception influenced debate, and altered reality, inspiring strict censorship legislation both within Europe and in the places that its nations colonised, where presses were strictly limited in their output, if not banned outright. Sir Roger L'Estrange – a true enemy of freedom of speech as it was conceived of in the seventeenth century – wrote from London in 1660 that ' it has been made a Question long agoe, whether more mischieve than advantage were not occasion'd to the Christian world by the invention of typography'. For L'Estrange, the answer was to destroy the equipment of subversive publishers when he was able to discover their hidden print shops in East London, and imprison any who sought to print outside of a strict system of licensing and patents. But in spite of his exhaustive personal efforts as the chief Licensor of the Press, he completely failed to stop the explosion of pamphlets and broadsides that came to characterise the industry in the second half of the seventeenth century.[6]

fig. 2
The interior of a
16th-century printing
press. Etching
(illustration to an
unidentified pub-
lication) after Jost
Amman, c. 1550–1650.

Aside from its mobilisation within a supernatural struggle between good and evil, the printing press could spread fairly quickly because its basic features – which together created an impression through a kind of screw press – were derived from a mix of recognisable tools and their associated skills. Gutenberg was a goldsmith – a trade well known for stamping and creating impressions, in addition to working with the kind of moulds that could be used to cast moveable type – and the printing press was essentially a modified wine press. Roger Chartier and Guglielmo Cavallo have argued that the major technological revolution was not the invention of printing, but a conceptual shift that came long before printing in Europe: the movement from scroll-based information to the codex or bound book, a process initiated by the third-century CE adoption of Christianity across the Roman

fig. 3
Portrait of Johannes Gutenberg, holding a type for the letter 'A' in his right hand and a block with the printed alphabet in the left. Etching and engraving, c. 1600–1680.

fig. 4
Illustration of a composing stick, from Joseph Moxon, *Mechanick exercises, or, The doctrine of handy-works: applied to the art of printing*. London: Joseph Moxon, 1683 (plate 24).

fig. 3

fig. 4

Empire.[7] The codex had been the chief information technology of early Christians – other 'books' of the Greek and Roman traditions were nearly always scrolls of papyrus, parchment or paper.

The invention of paper itself was crucial to the rapid multiplication of printed matter. That is attributed to the imperial Chinese dignitary Cai Lun in the second century CE; paper travelled along the Silk Road and eventually entered the material world of Europe via Islamic traders in the Middle East and Northern Africa. In that sense, the book was made possible only by a global economy. By the fourteenth century paper was being produced in Italy in imitation of its Eastern predecessors, and by the fifteenth century there were paper mills across Europe, stimulating a healthy trade in the rags and old clothing from which paper was made. The final component, in addition to well-worn trade routes and paper mills, was the longstanding tradition of annual fairs at which books produced by scribes – largely in scriptoria within monasteries and located near universities – were sold across Europe. Thus, both the raw material of book production and the audience for its consumption were well in place by the time Gutenberg was being sued in court by his financial backer, Johann Fust, for failing to make money from the invention. Both were thriving in 1456 when a court stripped Gutenberg of his press and his books and awarded them to Fust.[8] The true drama of the printing press as it spread from Fust's print shop in Mainz would be its scale of production, and its relocation of *where* knowledge could be produced – out of the monasteries and into the streets.

If that movement seems like a utopian generalisation, it was made good by the fact that every revolutionary, utopian movement since has had its advance guard of printers. It is possible to track revolutionary thinking along the lines of printed matter – heretics and upstarts have had to take the means of production into their own hands in the face of censorship and violence in just about every major social movement in the aftermath of printing: from Martin Luther's break with the Roman Catholic Church, to the Anabaptist break with Martin Luther, to the radical religious, anti-monarchical outpouring of late seventeenth-century England, to the output of revolutionary France, America and Haiti in the eighteenth century.

While the eighteenth century tends to be characterised as a time of secularisation, alongside the legal codification of many aspects of printing in ways that are recognisable to us today in terms of the rise of a mass-market publishing industry and the creation of author-centric copyright, the language of heaven, hell, plague and contested purity remained rife in descriptions of the output of the press.

William Blake, a great reader of earlier generations of mystics and spiritual seekers, drew from them in his own visionary, illuminated books when he described the 'Printing house in Hell' in *The Marriage of Heaven and Hell*, and, like Foxe in his *Book of Martyrs*, sought to turn the language of superstition on its head, this time by embracing the hellish nature of book production:

> I was in a Printing house in Hell & saw the method in which knowledge is transmitted from generation to generation. In the first chamber was a Dragon-Man, clearing away the rubbish from a caves mouth; within, a number of Dragons were hollowing the cave, In the second chamber was a Viper folding round the rock & the cave, and others adorning it with gold silver and precious stones. In the third chamber was an Eagle with wings and feathers of air, he caused the inside of the cave to be infinite, around were numbers of Eagle like men, who built palaces in the

immense cliffs. In the fourth chamber were Lions of flaming fire raging around & melting the metals into living fluids. In the fifth chamber were Unnam'd forms, which cast the metals into the expanse. There they were reciev'd by Men who occupied the sixth chamber, and took the forms of books & were arranged in libraries.[9]

On the one hand, Blake was describing his own unique printing practice: chamber one's 'clearing away' process describes preparing the plate for engraving; the second chamber of 'adorning' refers to the design of the plate itself; the third chamber cryptically refers to the process of etching using acid; the fourth adds 'fluids' or ink that would react with the acid through partial burning; the fifth is the method of printing on the press itself – casting metal 'into the expanse'; and the sixth chamber is where these printed sheets were bound into books by Blake and his wife, Catherine. At the same time, thinking through the activities undertaken at the 'Printing house in Hell' also doubled as an exercise or guided meditation describing the manifestation of unconscious thought into conscious action: printing as a mystical art, printing as an imitation of natural cognitive functions. Within Blake's topsy-turvy cosmology, Hell is where it's at. Heaven represents stagnancy, where 'Reason, call'd Good, is alone from the Soul', and Hell represents 'Energy' – the flow of creativity and innovation; 'Energy', for Blake, 'is Eternal Delight.'

Blake's use of printing to produce small, antagonistic works that criticised the rise of commodity culture, publishing as an industry, and industrialisation as a destructive force within Britain was prophetic. Later generations would look to him and his wife as the originators of artists' books and the small press, made in reaction to the industrialisation of printing processes, particularly the use of steam power in rotary presses beginning in the nineteenth century. Printing by manual labour, in smaller workshops, drawing from methods and tools dating back to the fifteenth and sixteenth centuries, retained an aura of radical potential that was picked up by the utopian idealists of the Arts and Crafts movement.

In spite of changes to the machinery, the creation of plates, the ecology of paper production, and the generally mind-boggling passage of time and development of digital technology, much of the attitude towards print has carried through to haunt each generation of printmakers and information activists. In times of conflict, information networks are still shut down and books are still burned, libraries and archives and museums are still bombed, and the language of infection and corruption is still levied against those who would dare speak or print truth to power. Across six centuries of impressing ink upon paper, the old superstitions still haunt and claw at us, and must be met in kind with more printing, more distribution, more books, at the hands of more and varied artisans and craftspeople.

Brooke Palmieri is a writer, printer and bookseller specialising in the history of gender non-conformity and LGBTQIA+ activism. After completing a PhD in the radical, communally driven printing practices of seventeenth-century Quakers, in 2018 they founded CAMP BOOKS as a combination of all their interests: writing and teaching about printing history, and building collections related to queer history and allied social movements. For more, see: http://campbooks.biz.

1 Filippo de Strata, *Polemic against Printing*, trans. Shelagh Grier with an introduction by Martin Lowry (Birmingham, The Hayloft Press, 1986).
2 For a sustained study of gender, sex and the construction of authorship, see Wendy Wall, *The Imprint of Gender: Authorship and Publication in the English Renaissance* (Cornell, NY: Cornell University Press, 1993). While she is writing about generations of writers and printers working a century later and thousands of miles away from those castigated in de Strata's letter, Wall shows how these men and women justified their work through a highly sexualised language – how 'the scene of writing was eroticized and scandalized'. See also Jeffrey Masten, *Textual Intercourse: Collaboration, Authorship, and Sexualities in Renaissance Drama* (Cambridge: Cambridge University Press, 1997).

3 *The Atlas of Early Printing* maps and visualises the spread of printing between 1450 and 1500. See https://atlas. lib.uiowa.edu/. As the scholar Kristen Poole writes, 'Anti-sectarian literature is infested with figurative accounts of teeming bees, frogs, locusts, serpents, eels, and maggots' (*Radical Religion from Shakespeare to Milton: Figures of Nonconformity in Early Modern England* [Cambridge: Cambridge University Press, 2000], 15, 104).
4 For more on this, see Walter D. Mignolo, *The Darker Side of the Renaissance: Literacy, Territoriality, and Colonization* (Ann Arbor: University of Michigan Press, 2003).
5 *The Acts and Monuments of John Foxe*, intro. George Townsend, ed. Stephen Reed Cattley, vol. 3 (London: R.B. Seeley and W. Burnside, 1837), 718–22.
6 Elizabeth Eisenstein, *Divine Art, Infernal Machine* (Philadelphia: University of Pennsylvania Press, 2011), 34.

7 Roger Chartier, *The Order of Books: Readers, Authors, and Libraries in Europe between the Fourteenth and Eighteenth Centuries* (Stanford, CA: Stanford University Press, 1994); Guglielmo Cavallo and Roger Chartier, eds, *A History of Reading in the West*, trans. Lydia Cochrane (Amherst, MA: University of Massachusetts Press, 1999).
8 Gutenberg's famous association with moveable type is a product of nationalistic debates over the invention that began in the sixteenth century and raged during the nineteenth. Documents linking him to the press in detail are few and far between, and are collected in Karl Schorbach's *The Gutenberg Documents, with Translations of the Texts into English* (Oxford: Oxford University Press, 1941).
9 Plate 15 in William Blake, *The Marriage of Heaven and Hell* (1790), The William Blake Archive, http://www.blakearchive. org/work/mhh.

Éditions du Livre

'A child has the power to remind us that colours or simple geometric shapes can be the main subject of a book. It teaches us to look at the world with new eyes,' says Alexandre Chaize (born in Lyon, France), who specialises in the publication of children's books.

Having grown up in the countryside, he says 'I kept a taste for simple things and timeless subjects that are found today in the works I publish: the moon, the sun, animals, fruits and vegetables.' Chaize studied at the École supérieure des arts décoratifs de Strasbourg, followed by a postgraduate degree at the École nationale supérieure des Beaux-Arts de Lyon. Life then took him to Madagascar, Paris and Brittany, where at one point he considered becoming an organic market gardener. He is now based in Strasbourg.

View of the exhibition Les Petits Spécimens – Mon tout est un livre, at Le Signe, Centre National Du Graphisme, Chaumont.

He describes himself as a publisher, initiating projects and then acting as a link between artists, printers, bookshops and readers. 'What I like most about this work is trying to create a graphic universe that is almost like a utopian language. A world of colours without words that could be compared to the world of music,' Chaize says of his work.

He publishes artists' books for children in the tradition of the Italian artist Bruno Munari (1907–98). 'For me, he is the author who invented the whole vocabulary of contemporary children's books: the play with folds, paper textures, transparencies and perforations that can be found in any children's book today. In my works, the narrative is born from the dialogue between the image and the manipulation of the book object. I defend an obvious principle: the form of the book is the content,' says Chaize.

He publishes books that are complex and costly to produce, and that do not conform to the usual rules. 'There is almost never a title on the cover of my books and the stories they tell are without text. You have to get in touch with the book object to understand its uniqueness,' Chaize explains.

The creative process of each of Chaize's projects starts with the artist's idea. Once he has decided to publish the book, Chaize will intervene very little in its overall concept, but do everything he can to reinforce it by finding the appropriate form. 'For me, the book is not a reproduction medium, but the work itself. So every detail is important: the choice of format, paper, printing process, binding. Everything is done so that the reader has a unique reading experience,' he says. For Chaize, this begins with the cover, which, as he describes, is 'often enigmatic, intriguing and inviting'. Information that is typically at the front of the book, such as the title and the author's name, is given instead in the colophon at the end of the book, like a closing credit. 'I remember a little girl leafing through *Dans la lune* by Fanette Mellier, the cover of which is decorated with a gilded circle. She looked at me while discovering the first pages of the book and suddenly exclaimed, "It's the moon!" This succession of circles had become the beginning of a story for her,' he recalls.

For Chaize, the book is, above all, a playful object. 'It is not sacred. Sometimes you have to cut it up, destroy it,' he says. This is the case of *Zoo in My Hand* by Inkyeong and Sunkyung Kim.

He sees the book as a playground for experimentation: paper, ink, binding, cover, gilding. Each of the works he publishes explores an attribute of the book, from the folds and cuts of Antonio Ladrillo's *Dots, Lines, Colours* to the thinness and transparency of the paper used in Fanette Mellier's *Aquarium*.

Some of his proudest moments to date include being invited in 2020 by Jean-Michel Géridan, the director of Le Signe – Centre national du graphisme, in Chaumont, to create Les Petits Spécimens 4 – an exhibition aimed at a young audience. This gave Chaize the opportunity to rethink the works as installations that were deployed in Le Signe's gallery. 'Thus, the parade of animals in *Zoo in My Hand* welcomed children, the colourful garden in *Hello Tomato* was transformed into a card game on a human scale, while *Matriochka* became a giant hut. You could literally walk into the books!' he says.

'I use masking tape every day to pack orders. So I asked Fanette Mellier to create personalised washi tapes for Éditions du Livre.'

Matriochka, Fanette Mellier, 2020 (second edition). Sixteen Russian dolls shrink from page to page, the last one measuring only a few millimetres high. Fanette Mellier invites us to explore this multicoloured family in microscopic detail. Observed under a magnifying glass, the ordinarily imperceptible details of the printing become the motifs that cover the tiny figurines. This book, in which hot gilding skips a generation, speaks of singularity and transmission.

Lines, Antonio Ladrillo, 2020 (second edition). Based on the same cuts, folds and coloured sequence, *Dots*, *Lines* and *Colors* only have one difference: their pattern, which is composed of dots, lines or blocks of colour that in the end modify our visual perception. Each book thus reveals its own dynamics and allows us to explore endless combinations of reading, in 2D or 3D.

Au soleil, Fanette Mellier, 2020 (second edition). *Au soleil* transcribes a daily solar cycle in six colours. Fanette Mellier proposes to assess the radiation of light as colour expansion: from morning blue to sunset purple, sun haloes permeate the atmosphere with incandescent colours.

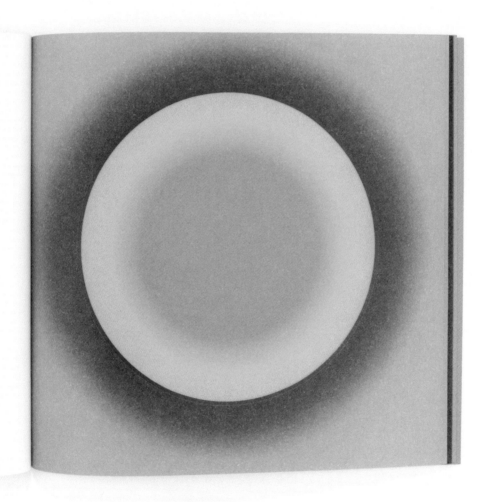

View of the exhibition Les Petits Spécimens – Mon tout est un livre, at Le Signe, Centre National Du Graphisme, Chaumont.

I defend an obvious principle:
the form of the book is the content.

Three Star Books

From left to right: Mélanie Scarciglia, Maddalena Quarta and Christophe Boutin in the studio, 2021.

At the age of fifteen Christophe Boutin (who was born in France) was already laying the groundwork for his future in publishing, attending a printing school, the École Estienne in Paris, before going on to study at the illustrious École des Arts décoratifs for two years. After playing music in the punk years, he eventually became a visual artist and also helped out at the Florence Loewy bookshop and gallery in the French capital. The store was dedicated to books by artists, and Boutin spent ten years there before moving on to publishing artists' books at the turn of the millennium. As Boutin puts it, 'I used to make art for many years and moved my ego to be at the service of Three Star Books.' Craftsmanship is at the centre of Three Star Books's activities, whose goal is to find the technical solutions that will enable artists to realise their vision. The publishers consider their projects to be very niche within the art publishing world: Three Star

Books typically makes very small editions as the books require bespoke production processes and the market is limited.

Three key people run the house – Mélanie Scarciglia managing sales, Maddalena Quarta and Christophe Boutin taking care of production. Boutin explains that they have a very collaborative approach to decision making: 'The three of us have intense exchanges when it comes to inviting an artist to publish a book and taking the right decisions when producing the project.' They always try to have their minds open to new experiences and visions. The trio call Paris their base, but work with an international team of producers, printers and manufacturers/makers of many sorts.

When it comes to production, Three Star Books has no boundaries. As a skilled studio dedicated to the production of books by artists they have decided to publish, they help the artists to alight on the right solution for every step of the process. At the very beginning of any new project, they hold conversations with the artists in order to help them clarify in what direction they want to go. 'Some artists have clear ideas, but with others it can take more time to really transform their vision into a book – but that's all the fun of being a publisher. Each new project is a new mountain to climb. Our books are conceived as artworks by the artists themselves and we provide the technical help,' Boutin explains.

Recently, they have made a project with the French artist Elvire Bonduelle that involves revisiting the celebrated Jacomet process, which used a combination of

AA Bronson, *After General Idea*, 2018. Edition of 40 copies.

stencils and collotype. 'Daniel Jacomet', Boutin relates, 'was the printer involved in outstanding projects by Sonia Delaunay, Henri Matisse, Le Corbusier, Picasso, and many other artists of that era. It has been challenging for us to reimagine a contemporary version of this forgotten combination of techniques.'

Scarciglia, Quarta and Boutin find inspiration for their publishing work by simply living a contemporary life. They believe that, from a publisher's perspective, the more you know the better you can help artists to make the right choices when it comes to creating a new work of art – in this instance, a book. Boutin says, 'Books are inspiring as a medium. We are lucky to never make the same object. Artists have their unique dreams, and we are here to make these a reality.' The team at Three Star Books achieve this by mixing new and old technologies, and they are committed to the belief that each project carries within itself its own inner production method: their mission is to reveal it in order to come as close as possible to the artist's dream.

Boutin barely considers his work as work: 'When you like what you do, working is not about working. There are tasks that can be boring, but these workaday moments are quickly erased when the new project you are working on takes shape.'

Sylvie Fleury, *Cuddly Book*, 2018. Edition of 10 copies.

Books are inspiring as a medium. We are lucky: we never make the same object twice. Artists have their unique dreams and we are here to make these a reality.

Elvire Bonduelle, *SO FAR SO GOOD*, 2021. Edition of 24 copies.

Blake Rayne, *Almanac*, 2013. Edition of 10 copies, co-published with Westreich/Wagner Publications.

Candor Arts

Candor Arts is a joint project between Matt Austin (born in Hartford, Connecticut, USA) and Melanie Teresa Bohrer (born in Lucerne, Switzerland). Two self-taught bookbinders, they are interested in the power-shifting capabilities of artists' book publishing. The main purpose of their project is to provide fair publishing opportunities for artists.

The duo invests in artists dedicated to up-lifting communities who have been dispro-portionately harmed and exploited within their industry and society. In most cases, this involves the authors sharing their own personal narratives of learning and healing from traumas they have endured. Each book is a collaboration that is built on trust and a willingness to be open and learn from one another. Through learning about the life and background that informs the work of each artist, Candor guides the design process, while the artist retains full control of the content that exists in the book.

As Bohrer explains it, Candor wishes to 'reject the status quo of book publishing, which thrives by following the same patterns of capitalism, inevitably fostering a toxic, unsustainable culture of competition/individualism, white supremacy, profit over the wellness of people, labour exploitation, and hierarchies of subjugation'. She continues: 'Our publishing models offer an alternative that prioritises care for the artist and considers the impact of this collaboration in the context of what other modes of support they may need outside of art-making.'

For Austin, the whole cultural identity of books and publishing – the concept that published content holds weight and importance – offers potential for fostering a more equitable society. 'By engaging in publishing work from a place of intention, care and awareness for the injustices we contribute to through complicity, lived experiences that have been systemically silenced and made invisible in our society can be heard, learned from, and ultimately, valued through experiences with books,' he says.

He argues that in Western societies there is a constant resistance to alternative social systems created in response to inequity. But, in the case of books, there is still an existing social system – libraries – where access to learning can be free and equitable. In his eyes this system mostly still exists 'without incentive to generate capital or uphold white supremacy'. And, in the realm of artists' books, there are not only libraries where all people can access the work and learn from it for free but also cultural institutions, art book fairs, galleries, social media platforms, artist talks, book clubs, book stores, private collections, public collections.

However, Austin believes that the current norms of publishing mostly fail and exploit authors and artists, particularly artists and authors who are not white men. 'Publishing is a social concept that has been massively incentivised – mostly at the expense of the author – to generate capital and uphold white supremacy. We, as well as many other independent publishers, are working towards equitable systems of publishing against this standard, with care for people, not profit, as the main focus. This network we share as people imagining an equitable society – and working towards it – is what makes

Matt Austin (left) and Melanie Teresa Bohrer (right) amidst production of *the other option is to slow down* by Amanda Williams.

books inspiring to me – that there is so much power and capacity within books and the communities created around them,' he says.

Candor Arts' creative process typically begins with a conversation with the artist about their work and the intentions they have for creating an edition. It is crucial that they know from the outset of a project what function the book should have in the world, as this determines its price point and thereby its production techniques. 'So to some extent we begin with the end and then move back to the beginning,' Bohrer explains.

After some discussion, they begin to spend some time with the content. If possible, Bohrer and Austin prefer to visit with the artists and authors in the physical space or location where the work was created, in order to have the mood, light, colour and feeling become part of their aesthetic decisions when designing and producing the work. While creating the digital file, they will simultaneously look at material swatches to start thinking about the physicality of the object as this affects the way in which it is created and represented digitally. 'The time of production of an edition can vary greatly depending on its complexity. Some projects will take years to make, others take days. Similarly the production expenses also vary immensely,' Bohrer says.

Once a complete sample has been created, they usually like to share it online as a pre-order item, in order to start recouping the investment that they fronted for the production. 'As the work sells, we are in communication with the artist about how close they are to breaking even in the costs we fronted for the production of the work. We track inventory to let them know where the work has been placed (usually institutions and private patrons) as well as keep records of accounts to make sure that we split sales return 50/50 after both equal shares of production expenses have been met,' Bohrer explains.

When it comes to techniques and materials, Austin says he gets most excited when they are doing something that would otherwise be impossible or very difficult using typical mass production techniques. 'Maybe having a machine do something it wasn't designed to do or learning that a certain material can work in place of the traditional manufactured material. So, I guess the equipment that most often allows us to experiment would be our Kensol foil stampers, our consumer inkjet printer, and, of course, our hands,' he says.

Candor Arts team members Katie Chung (left) and Hannah Batsel (right) at work in the West Town studio.

Melanie Teresa Bohrer opening the special edition of Barbara Jones-Hogu's *RESIST, RELATE, UNITE*.

The network we share as people imagining an equitable society – and working toward it – is what makes books inspiring to me: that there is so much power and capacity within books and the communities created around them.

Artist Amanda Williams monoprinting the covers of her book
the other option is to slow down in the Candor Arts studio.

Book Works

Book Works building, 19 Holywell Row.

Founded in London's Borough Market in 1984 by bookbinders Jane Rolo and Rob Hadrill, Book Works is a contemporary arts organisation with a unique role as makers and publishers of books. Its founders believe that books are a perfect vehicle for sharing information, and the democracy of books as a means of distributing knowledge is one reason why they began publishing. The opportunity to put work out into the world that might not otherwise have seen the light of day is another.

Book Works began life as a platform for artists' books. It began with organising exhibitions and publishing a newsletter detailing various artists' book events in London and further afield, such as the Frankfurt Book Fair. To fund the organisation, Rolo and Hadrill also ran a bookbinding service and eventually began publishing artists' books.

Book Works occupies a special place in the culture of publishing, offering a space to both art and writing of a kind not usually found in the more mainstream publishing world. The studio offers a specialist service for artists, designers, galleries and businesses, while as a publisher it focuses on commissioning new work by emerging artists or writers. It is important for the studio that these publications reach a wide public, whether through mainstream distribution networks or through informal networks.

The studio and publishing arms of the organisation run education events – including bookbinding classes, artists' surgeries, lectures and workshops. The two arms collaborate on many projects together, on educational activities and the commission and fabrication of special editions and prints. These include handbound books by Lubaina Himid, Katrina Palmer and Susan Hiller, as well as specialist cases like the Perspex case the studio developed with Liam Gillick to house a special edition of *All Books*, each one published with an individually coloured drawing on the cover.

Auras and Levitations (2008, second edition 2010) by Susan Hiller.

Envy by Douglas Gordon.

Book Works commissions projects in various ways. It has at least one open submission every year to cast the net wider and find out about artists and writers outside of its immediate community. It never publishes books that are already produced, instead choosing to work with artists to develop a project in collaboration. For Book Works, the time spent developing projects with artists is the most important part of the process.

Book Works caters to a broad and diverse community, from running workshops for students to developing bespoke boxes and bindings for artists, photographers, galleries and publishers. Clients range from artists with whom they have enjoyed a long relationship to artists or galleries working with them for the first time. Most of these relationships are nurtured over time and through word-of-mouth recommendations.

One of the most rewarding aspects of its work is seeing the relationship it has with its readers. Book Works strives to engage audiences in what it does, whether that is through projects in libraries, readings, workshops, or performance events and lectures. It is driven by the desire to put ideas out into the world that are challenging, or which might not otherwise have found a platform.

The Library Was
(2015, second
edition 2018)
by OOMK.

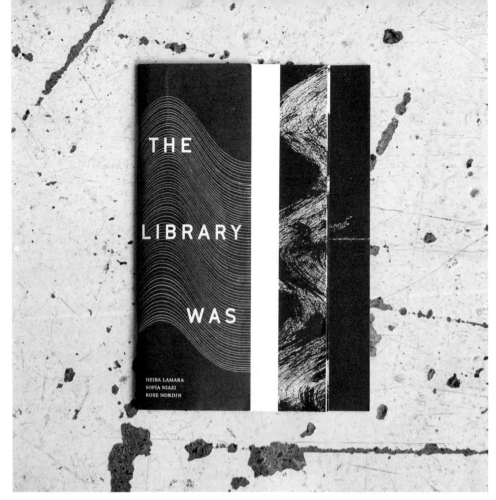

*Upcycle This
Book* (2017)
by Gavin Wade.

The democracy of books as a means of distributing knowledge is part of why we began publishing.

Sheryl Oppenheim

Sheryl Oppenheim (born in Florida, USA) first became interested in artists' books when she was studying for a year in Rome. Attending the opening of a Bruno Munari exhibition at the Museo dell'Ara Pacis, she saw examples of his *Libro Letto* ('bed/read book') series – giant pieces of coloured material sewn into pillows-cum-books – and for the first time was struck by the book as an object and as a 'container for strange ideas beyond written words'.

The next formative period in her career came during her first job in New York at Talas, a bookbinding supplier in Brooklyn. It was here that she began to learn the basics of bookbinding and began to practise the craft herself. In 2011 she began marbling paper, and by 2016 she was learning Suminagashi ('floating ink'), the Japanese form of this art.

She considers herself both a painter and paper marbler: 'I approach paper marbling from painting, as far as it involves colour, composition, emotions, thoughts, and a sense of time.' Today, she works out of a 400-square-foot studio in a historic building called the Brooklyn Army Terminal, in the Brooklyn neighbourhood of Sunset Park. The space is run by an organisation called Chashama, and about 20 other artists have studios there. Oppenheim works alone, without any assistants, but she does collaborate with book studio Small Editions and the bookbinder Sarah Smith in the making of her books.

Oppenheim explains why books inspire her: 'I like the physical experience of holding a book and turning the pages. I think it is a great way to show art, a great way to look at and interact with it. It's more personal.' She has a great appreciation for the privacy and the comfort of sitting with and going through a book at your own pace. 'I can't help but notice that even a photograph of a book, the way it exists as an object in space, is more compelling than a photo of a painting. You relate to it in a different way,' she adds.

When it comes to her process, Oppenheim firmly believes that having a grasp of craft facilitates her ability to make art. She teaches her students the same when it comes to marbling, encouraging them to first understand the rules, to understand where the limits are, before breaking them. She thinks of knowing how to make a book as being like knowing how to build a house. 'That's true of marbling paper. It's true of the collages I make now, which take the cutting, hinging and gluing

techniques I learned from bookbinders. And having an understanding of paper, choosing the right materials in that way … that really helps me to make art,' she explains.

Oppenheim's practice differs significantly from that of a craftsperson, particularly as marbling is, in fact, considered a trade. She has chosen not to focus on producing runs of nearly identical papers, although she has a deep respect for the mastery involved in the practice of the trade. 'When I marble I am looking for something, trying to reveal something not yet known, trying to surprise myself, and trying to articulate myself. If I'm anything, I'm a printmaker, albeit a messy one.'

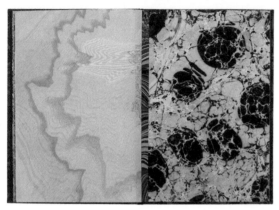

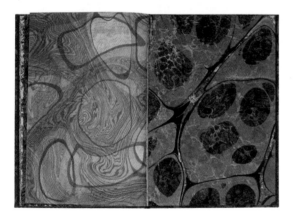

Top: from *Touching*, 2018, acrylic and Suminagashi marbling on hand-made cotton and washi papers.
Middle and bottom: from *Hard to Say*, 2019, acrylic and Suminagashi marbling on handmade cotton and washi papers.

She works predominantly with size-based marbling and Suminagashi marbling, and the papers are often made into books where the marbling serves not as the endpapers but as the content. Recently, Oppenheim began to make marble collages using a coloured washi paper called Yatsuo. She has many favourite materials, but paper is as important to her as paint. For marbling in the Western style, she loves using Arches Velin Johannot paper. She believes the materials you start with really make a difference. For Suminagashi, she prefers the Sekishu papers made by Osamu Hamada and So Kubota.

Oppenheim draws inspiration for her art from many sources: 'It's like a soup of all the things I've looked at and experienced and thought about. I think a lot about strangeness. I always love to notice when I'm looking at something odd.'

Oppenheim's artist books are in numerous public collections, including the Metropolitan Museum of Art's Thomas J. Watson Library, the Walker Art Center, the New York Public Library, the Brooklyn Museum and the National Museum of Women in the Arts. She has participated in exhibitions at the Minnesota Center for Book Arts, Sadie Halie Projects, Deanna Evans Projects, International Print Center New York, Small Editions and the Cranbrook Museum of Art.

Oppenheim is marbling with acrylic paint. This technique of applying successive drops of colour
to create more or less balanced bullseyes is what she uses as a starting point for combed patterns.

When I marble I am looking for something, trying to reveal something not
yet known, trying to surprise myself,
and trying to articulate myself.

Trying (Unmarbled), 2021, Japanese paper collage, 38 x 51 cm.

SHERYL OPPENHEIM

Beginners Luck, 2021, acrylic marbling on Japanese paper collage, 38 x 51 cm.

Inka Bell

With a background in graphic design, Inka Bell (born in Espoo, Finland) is a visual artist who works predominantly in printmaking. Several years ago, when she was seeking to gain some perspective on her artistic work, she undertook an MFA at the Academy of Fine Arts in Helsinki, where she has lived for the last 20 years.

Bell is currently setting up a new studio, having recently moved there from a shared environment. She recognises that she needs more space and a place where she can be by herself to focus on her artistic work. Of her practice, she explains, 'I think "visual artist" would describe me the best, although I feel like many of the techniques I use are not too far from a craftsperson's methods. I often say that I work in the expanded field of printmaking, and for me, that means a certain experimental way of using techniques and materials.'

Bell's work is purely non-representational and minimalistic, focusing on observing the behaviour of the physical and abstract space of the material, and the process of her chosen media. In her practice, she explores the relationship between two-dimensional and three-dimensional, through material, colour, surface and repetition. She is inspired by the way a book feels and smells when you pick it up. Paper, in particular, drives her creative process, and she uses it for printing or shaping into new forms. 'I somehow enjoy the mundane aspect of it. I also love the fragile yet stubborn nature of the material,' she says.

Bell has embraced new technologies and considers them an essential part of her process. Her practice typically involves some form of dialogue with a machine, whether it's a computer to create the matrix or a tool that enables her to work the material in a way that she could not have achieved with her hands alone. Ultimately, though, it is her hands that refine and revise what the machine has shaped.

In the past two years, she has begun working with a laser cutter which has opened up more possibilities of working with materials like paper. Part of her practice involves creating three-dimensional works – paper sculptures – in a process vaguely reminiscent of weaving. 'In these works, I am particularly interested when two surfaces meet each other, forming entities that only appear when several hundred, sometimes thousands, of elements are layered together,' Bell remarks.

She has tried to understand machine coding and find innovative ways to use it. For example, in Bell's series *0:23–6:30 min*, the parameters of the laser cutter have been manipulated, so that the beam which is supposed to cut through the paper is altered to the point at which it solely 'draws' a digitally created line onto the surface, resembling a light pen stroke. Interrupting the process at certain times exposes the almost arbitrary order in which the machine draws, transferring an interpretation of human visual output into the machine's code. When the laser cuts through the paper, it leaves burnt edges that appear slightly three-dimensional. Bell elaborates: 'It is difficult to fully control the outcome, although it can be affected by altering the laser settings. Ultimately, an element of chance often remains. The laser cutter enables me to create shapes and structures that would otherwise be impossible for me to achieve.'

The stage where the work starts to find its form but is still open to anything new is the most rewarding for Bell, because it is something that cannot be planned for. She enjoys surprising herself. 'I think I'm letting go of the idea that something needs to be perfect (and what does perfect mean anyway?) and rather pursuing something that would not be.'

I somehow enjoy the mundane
aspect of paper. I also love the fragile,
yet stubborn nature of the material.

Detail of *Work 3*, 2020. Paper, metal stand, threaded rod, metal nuts, approx. 28 x 14 x 4 cm.

Composition 19, 2019. Screen print on coloured paper, approx. 11 x 13 x 3 cm.

INKA BELL

Composition 17, 2019. Screen print on coloured paper, approx. 11 x 11.5 x 3 cm.

CRAFT

Kathy Abbott

'I think humans have a fundamental need to use their hands and to make,' says Kathy Abbott (born in Enfield, UK), a bookbinder who puts craftsmanship at the heart of everything she does. Her long and varied training has given her a deep knowledge of her craft and was fundamental to forming her practice. As an apprentice bookbinder back in 1989 in a trade bindery in Enfield, London – where she grew up – she was the only female working in a team of sixty-five men. From there, she went on to study for a Higher National Diploma in Design Bookbinding at the London College of Printing (now London College of Communication), which she expanded upon with a BA Honours degree at University of Roehampton, now London. Working as a bindery manager for nine years at an antiquarian book dealers' broadened her knowledge immeasurably.

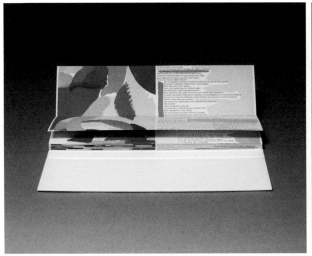
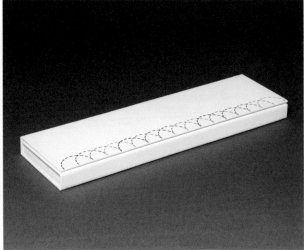

La Prose du Transsibérien et de la Petite Jehanne de France, Blaise Cendrars and Sonia Delaunay-Terk, recreated by Kitty Maryatt, Two Hands Press, 2018. A three-flap enclosure, held closed with magnets, covered in full alum-tawed goatskin with multicoloured onlays. Bound in 2019.

Abbott now works out of her studio in Westbourne Park, London, which she has shared with bookbinder and artist Tracey Rowledge since 2001 (see p. 154). Part of a converted garage, which was once a stable for horses, it sits in a quiet mews. 'It has great light and is very peaceful, although it's quite small; we utilise every crumb of space!' she says. She also teaches advanced-level Fine Binding at the City Lit, London, and conducts bookbinding workshops across the UK and overseas. She is a partner in Bench-mark Bindery, established in 2009 with Rowledge, a founding member of the group Tomorrow's Past, and is the author of *Bookbinding: A step-by-step guide*, published by The Crowood Press in 2010.

Abbott identifies as a bookbinder but also draws and makes relief prints. Of her practice she says: 'It has developed and grown by trial and error and, most importantly, trusting my gut instinct. It took me a good while to find "my voice" and to feel confident in it.' A minimalist at heart, she responds to the text, using materials to create a sensitive, abstract expression of the narrative content.

When approaching a new bookbinding project, she will first read the text a few times, take notes, and then let it sit for a while. She often gets inspiration when doing something mindless like walking back from the underground station, supermarket shopping, or in the 'magical' moments as she wakes up. Her ideas are then distilled down to their very essence, 'I try to express myself in as minimal a way as possible. Then I make maquettes or trial pieces to see how the idea works, and then I begin the binding process.'

She has a deep admiration for the mat-erials related to bookbinding, particularly

Sewing a multicoloured endband.

leather and vellum. Often, she will use the unique grain and markings of these materials as the basis of her response to a text. The early stages of the binding process are what inspire Abbott most – the preparation of the text-block, sewing, gilding, edge decoration, endbanding – and it is nature that is her biggest influence. She also looks to other disciplines such as art, ceramics, jewellery, textiles and printmaking, recognising the importance of looking outside the realm of bookbinding for inspiration.

She believes that the recent resurgence of craft can only be a good thing: 'The only way crafts continue and develop is through getting new blood, from all sorts of backgrounds.' Abbott herself enjoys making by hand but isn't resistant to new technologies if they could do something as well as, or better than, her.

Abbott describes her proudest moments to date: 'I am proudest of my students and what they achieve, and I was honoured to be awarded the Marsh Heritage Award for my teaching back in 2018. I have also been lucky enough to bind and repair some very important books: five different copies of Shakespeare's First Folio, and an Islamic manuscript dating back to the time of the Prophet Muhammad.'

My practice has grown by trial and error and, most importantly, trusting my gut instinct. It took me a good while to find 'my voice' and feel confident in it.

Hudibras. Samuel Butler, London, 1817. Adapted 'simplified binding'. Hand-decorated, handmade paper spine and hand-coloured, handmade paper over archival millboard boards. Bound in 2010.

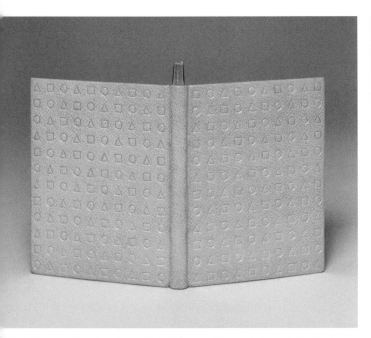

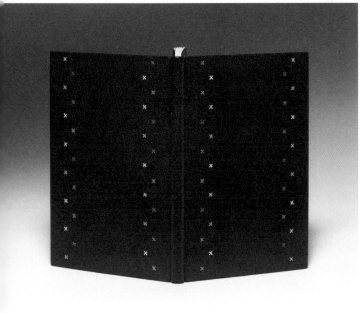

Top left: *The House, the Garden, and the Steeple*, Arthur L. Humphreys, first edition, London, 1906. Bound in full yellow goatskin with gold tooling, top edge gilded; coloured handmade paper endpapers and doublures. Bound in 2015.

Bottom left: *Poems and Pieces 1911 to 1961*, Francis Meynell, The Nonesuch Press, London, 1961. Bound in full chocolate goatskin with hand-cut multicoloured goatsin onlays; Japanese handmade paper endpapers and doublures. Bound in 2011.

Centre: The endpapers and doublures of *Unpublished Early Poems*, Alfred Lord Tennyson (ed. Charles Tennyson, his grandson), Macmillan & Co. Ltd, London, 1931. A stub-binding bound in full grey goatskin over sculpted boards, cold gilded with Caplain gold leaf, top edge gilded with Caplain gold leaf; hand-decorated handmade paper endpapers and doublures. Bound in 2019.

KATHY ABBOTT

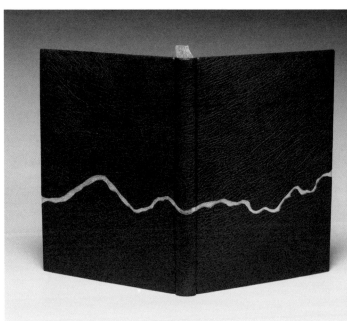

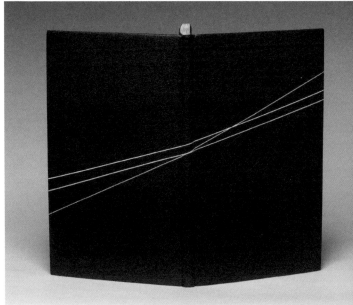

Top right: *Down the River*. H.E. Bates, wood engravings by Agnes Miller Parker. Victor Gollanz, 1937. Bound in full navy blue goatskin with recessed white gilded detail, top edge gilded in white gold; coloured handmade paper endpapers and doublures. Bound in 2009.

Bottom right: *New York Revisited.* Kenneth Auchincloss, wood engravings by Gaylord Shanilec, The Grolier Club of New York, 2002. Bound in full black goatskin with handmade paper onlays, top edge coloured; coloured handmade paper endpapers and doublures. Bound in 2008.

Kate Brett

Kate Brett (born in Dorking, UK) designs and makes marbled papers. She grew up in the south of England, spent 20 years in Scotland, then 15 in Cambridge, before recently relocating her studio to Scotland, where she had gone to university. Throughout her career she has set up her studios in some interesting and exciting locations, including in Africa where her husband, a rhino ecologist, was then working. She comments: 'I find that as long as the studio is not too cold, marbling will usually work in most places. One of the joys of marbling is that it is quite easy to transport because you just need a tray, some carrageen, papers and paints, and as long as the postal system works customers do not seem to mind where you are sending the parcel from.'

In the summer months, Brett and her family spend a lot of time in the Outer Hebrides where she will often work, collecting the carrageen seaweed from the rocks and drying it for use later. She says, 'This is fine. The only thing is, you have to get to the post office by 9.30 in the morning or the parcels will miss the boat.'

Brett taught herself marbling after being fascinated by the marbled papers she came across in old books while doing a course in bookbinding at Guildford College. She spent many hours trying lots of different methods, so it was a case of trial and error. She was thrilled when, after many hours, the water-based paints floated on the carrageen jelly and she made some tentative speckled patterns. With encouragement from Gabrielle Falkiner of Falkiner Fine Papers, Brett then tried to reproduce some more traditional designs such as Old Dutch, Antique Spot and French Curl. This set her on the path she has followed ever since. As she describes, 'Trying

Brett laying down the paper onto an antique spot design.

to recreate some of the older patterns is the type of marbling I enjoy most … I find it very satisfying to produce papers that resemble some of these old designs from the early marblers in the eighteenth century.' To this day, she uses traditional methods of floating water-based paints on a size (jelly) made from carrageen moss.

The papers Brett creates are used in bookbinding as endpapers or on covers, but are also adapted for more novel uses such as lampshades and other decorative items. She has made designs over the years that she feels able to reproduce, so samples of these appear on her website. Customers then select which patterns they may like and order them directly. She also takes on commissions to design patterns for particular projects, as, for example, when she was asked to do a design to match the colours of a particular Picasso painting. This pattern was then

reproduced to be used as the endpapers in the catalogue for the *Picasso 1932* exhibition at Tate Modern in 2018.

Brett finds marbling both satisfying and exasperating: 'Even after 40 years I still have bad days and have to empty the size down the sink and start again. A full day of marbling can be exhausting, it being quite a backbreaking business. However, these setbacks are made worthwhile when the sheet you draw from the tray gives you pleasure and everything is behaving as it should.'

Her daughter has recently been helping her and learning about her work. She has now set up her own studio in Bristol where, apart from producing some fine papers, she is being innovative and experimental, marbling on more unusual materials such as linen and porcelain door knobs. 'I hope she will carry on,' Brett says.

Brett holding some carrageen which has been rinsed and dried ready to be boiled.

KATE BRETT

I find it satisfying to produce papers that resemble some of these old designs from the early marbles in the eighteenth century.

Above: Spattering spots of paint with a fan brush while creating an antique spot pattern.
Right: Using a comb to make the curls onto an 'Old Dutch' style pattern.

102   KATE BRETT

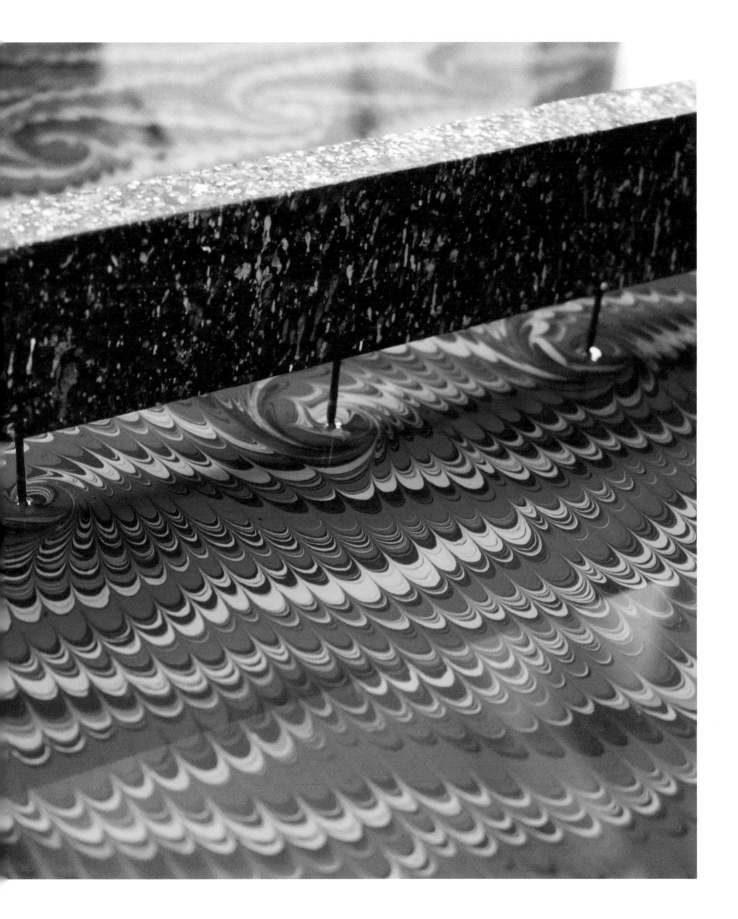

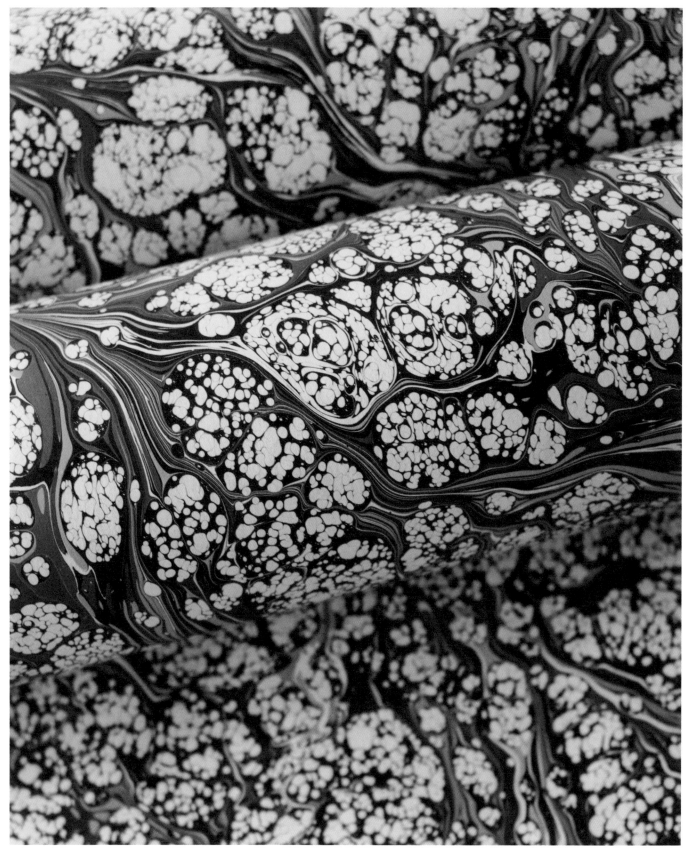

Gloster pattern.

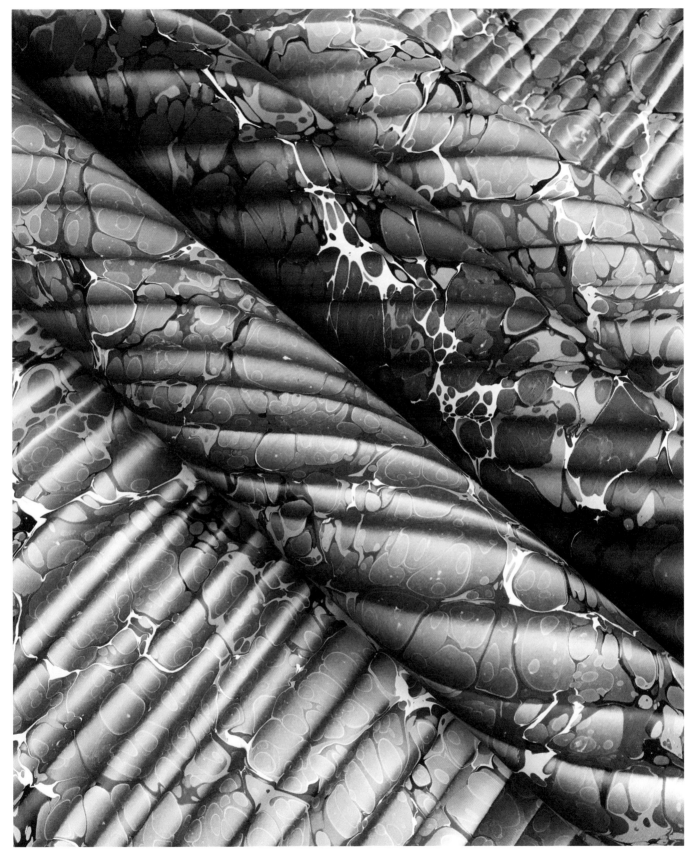

Spanish Wave.

Kamisoe

Ko Kado (born in Kyoto, Japan) is an artisan of the traditional printing technique of karakami, which involves decorative papermaking using woodblock prints. He is one of only around ten masters in Japan currently practising the craft. His atelier, Kamisoe (meaning 'to add something onto paper'), has occupied a 90-year-old former barbershop in the Nishijin district of Kyoto since 2009. It comprises a small ground-floor shop, complete with the original barbershop sink, and a first-floor studio, and sits among traditional textile workshops and teahouses. Kado creates screens, wallpaper, postcards, panels for fusuma sliding doors, and other com-missions such as artwork for book covers, album sleeves and event invitations.

Kado studied graphic design in San Francisco, before moving to New York to work in art production. He returned to his hometown of Kyoto to learn karakami in a centuries-old printing studio in the northern part of Kyoto, where he remained for five years. Nonetheless he says: 'I am mostly self-taught. There are currently very few, if any, opportunities to be taught the craft/technique. My practice developed through a combination of my own research and experimentation,' Kado explains.

Karakami is a type of woodblock printing that was introduced to Japan during the Nara period (710–94) from Tang China. The pigment is applied to a tool called a *furui* which is then applied to the woodblock relief surface. Washi – Japanese handmade paper – is then placed on top of the woodblock and burnished gently by hand. These two techniques

combined – the *gataoshi* (the indirect application of pigment onto the relief surface) and *tesuri* (hand burnishing) – result in the unique qualities of karakami. 'Historically, karakami was often used to illustrate and decorate books, and one of the most beautiful examples of this is the series of books called the *Sagabon*. I was responsible for the reproduction of the karakami covers for a reprint of the series in 2018,' says Kado.

Kado creates the pigments himself, but commissions local woodworkers to produce the blocks according to his original designs. Because he opened his own atelier, he did not have any old print blocks, so all the designs he uses are new for each project. This approach is distinct from other karakami printers, who typically use woodblocks inherited from previous masters.

His creations adorn Kyoto temples, teahouses, boutique hotels and private households alike. Tradition is important to Kado, but his designs are distinctive in their contemporary aesthetic, thanks to his background in graphic design. They are minimal, clean-lined, graphic and quintessentially Japanese. His process begins by 'researching pattern, form and colour, not only from nature, but from the human made like architecture and cityscapes. Then I make patterns and print them onto papers.'

White pigment on silver paper.

The ink is transferred to the tray.

The ink is mixed.

The ink is transferred onto the *furui*.

A sheet of washi paper is placed onto the woodblock and burnished by hand.

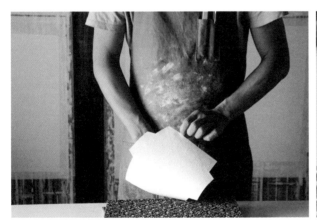

The washi paper is removed from the woodblock.

A woodblock.

I am mostly self-taught. There are currently very few, if any, opportunities to be taught this craft.

Esme Winter

Letterpress printing cards at LCBA.

Esme Winter (born in Bristol, UK) grew up in Bristol and Wiltshire, studying Textile Design at the University of the West of England Bristol. After relocating to London for some years, she set up her eponymous brand with her husband, Richard Sanderson (born in Norwich, UK), in 2011. They have since moved back to live and work in the south-west of England.

Winter describes herself as a designer first and foremost. She feels that she has returned to her roots, trusting her instincts and natural inclination to work with repeat pattern. Through her eponymous brand, the husband-and-wife team creates motifs, choosing the colours and material. The finished product is printed and manufactured by others, but carefully overseen by the pair.

Pattern design using hand-set letterpress type.

The designs evolve naturally, from drawing. It's a hands-on process, with every design starting life using pen and paper. At this very organic stage, Winter finds drawing patterns almost meditative, enabling her to keep a clear head and to work without distraction. She also finds it helpful to step away, revisiting and developing the design over time, since often the patterns will feel different from before. After this, she refines and plays with the scale, shape and colours. 'In this way, all of our patterns have almost had their own life. It's as if we have to give each pattern time to grow before trusting or finding its particular appeal. Sometimes it's very hard to apply a new design immediately – some of our "new" designs are years old!' says Winter.

In her branded products, Winter likes to use a range of processes and materials, and more often than not these will encompass time-honoured ways of working. For example, papers are printed using offset lithography, a traditional technique for commercial scale printmaking. The Curwen Press, at the vanguard of British printing in the early twentieth century, utilised an early form of offset lithography when working with Neo-Romantic artists like Edward Bawden, Eric Ravilious and Paul Nash. 'We hope to retain that feel,' says Winter. All Esme Winter cards are letterpress-printed, and Winter and her husband are involved from start to finish – from mixing inks and proofing samples, to the finished product. 'The people we work with mean a lot to our business. We use a selection of different paper stocks but always aim for those that are archival and ecologically sound, whether recycled papers or FSC approved. We also use vegetable-based inks, but this is almost universal in most printing presses these days. Ultimately, we're looking for a

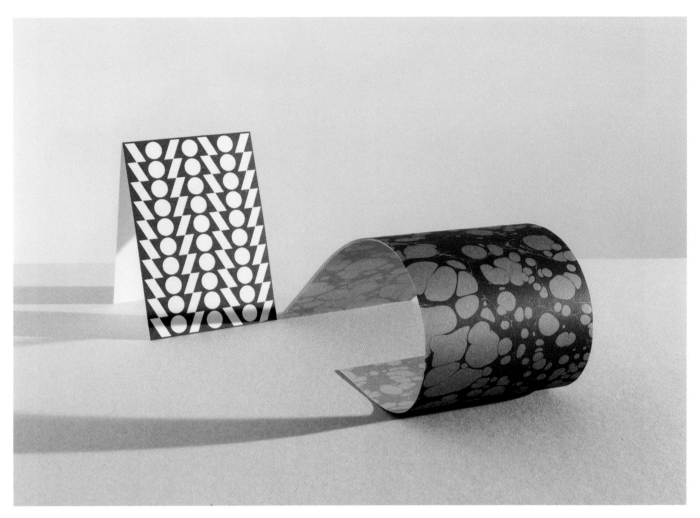

Pattern papers and cards.

All of our patterns have almost had their own life. It's as if we have to give each pattern time to grow before trusting or finding its particular appeal.

balance between texture and ink reaction when choosing papers. Our aim is to appreciate different technologies, materials and their possibilities,' she says.

A lot of Winter's initial inspiration comes from her family. Her parents run a specialist auction house which was, and still is, a treasure trove of influences. Rifling through books, decorative papers and beautiful ephemera fostered in her a natural appreciation for all things print, pattern and paper.

She is a big believer that pattern and colour can have a meaningful effect on our everyday surroundings, however small. Through her brand, she strives to create items that bring people joy, enrich the art of letter-writing, and inspire gift-giving. 'To send a heartfelt handwritten message, share a beautifully presented gift, or keep a special card on your mantelpiece is a wonderful thing. We want to encourage and enrich this honest, tactile way of communicating in our very digital world,' Winter shares.

Letterpress printing cards at LCBA.

Range of pattern paper books, journals and notebooks.

Handmade box covered with Esme Winter 'fantasy' marbled paper in emerald.

Émilie Fayet

Émilie Fayet was born in 1992 and grew up in Montjoie-en-Couserans in France, a little village in Ariège in the central Pyrenees. She studied graphic design at the École Estienne, Paris, and at the École supérieure d'art et design (ESAD) in Valence, before joining the Fotokino team in Marseille in 2017, where she worked for three years. At the same time, she developed her own practice, linked to ancient techniques for extracting vegetable dyes. By gathering wild plants in the city and its surroundings, she produces dyeing materials for paper and fabric.

She says of her practice: 'When the colours appear in the pot, it is quite magical and gives me the feeling of being some kind of alchemist or a witch. I find it incredible that plants can have so many secrets.'

During her graphic design studies she often experimented in the photographic laboratory and developed a taste for photosensitive images. One day Fayet came across anthotypes, a means of image reproduction discovered by Sir John Herschel, the inventor of the cyanotype, which consists of using plant juices to make photosensitive solutions. This discovery led her on to the world of vegetable dyes, and she began to wonder about possible alternatives to traditional graphic printing, particularly in the context of a strong revival in micro-publishing and artisanal crafts.

In 2016 Fayet collaborated with Michel Garcia, a vegetable dye manufacturer based in Lauris, in Vaucluse, on the development of three inks to be used in the printing of a graphic design project. 'Meeting Michel allowed me to discover

Fayet harvesting wild heather for dyeing.

Fayet dyeing textiles in her workshop.

Handkerchief project in collaboration with Alexis Poline, 2020.

a whole new world, and I was able to understand the issues at stake. With this project, I was able to get a real feel for the limits (but also the benefits) of this artisan approach in comparison with industrial techniques,' she recalls.

A few years later, Fayet trained in dyeing and cultivation in the Conservatory Garden of Tinctorial Plants of the Couleur Garance Association in Lauris. At the beginning, her research focused on paper inks, but gradually she drifted towards the world of textiles and became anchored in the region through learning about the local flora. 'Today, I try to design projects that maintain a balance between the quantity of raw materials, energy consumption, working time, and the quality of the result, in a bid to make my production viable, aesthetic and ethically responsible,' she says. 'Nowadays, I would be tempted to say that I am a designer with an artisanal practice, or an artisan with a designer's approach.'

Fayet's research focuses on issues of local territory and local resources. She is particularly interested in invasive plants and recycling, and tries to make her practice part of an ethical economy. By sharing this work with a wide range of audiences, she addresses issues such as environmental awareness and the valorisation of natural resources through art. Through their sensitive and poetic approach these encounters invite people to reconnect with their own territory and engage with it in a respectful way while refreshing their view of urban nature.

Fayet's speciality is the extraction of vegetable dyes, and for textiles she likes to experiment with different techniques and tools for applying mordants: screen printing, pads, brushes, rollers, sprays and pipettes. She sources her fabrics from second-hand shops. Alongside her harvesting practice, she also recovers different tinctorial vegetable extracts from particular retailers – such as kitchen waste and wood shavings.

Her creative process generally starts with looking for tinctorial plants according to the season and the area she is working in. 'When the time is right, I gather the raw material: I go for a walk and I harvest the plants. Then I imagine the project by going back and forth between the idea, the choice of techniques, shapes and colours,' she says. For Fayet, the final project has to make sense, and the content is just as important as the form. 'I then work out a timetable, as dyeing requires many stages, with varying lengths of time to wait between them. I do various tests and experiments before I set about the final production.'

She finds inspiration in the natural forms and colours she encounters in her local environment. 'I'm lucky enough to live in a city where the ultra-urban rubs shoulders with wild nature,' she says. 'Marseille floods us with a very special light, and I often find the colour of its rocks and its skies in my work,' she says.

A colour chart of dyed tests, using vegetable dyes harvested from Marseille wild plants.

Dyers chamomile screenprints, diploma project in collaboration with Michel Garcia, 2016.

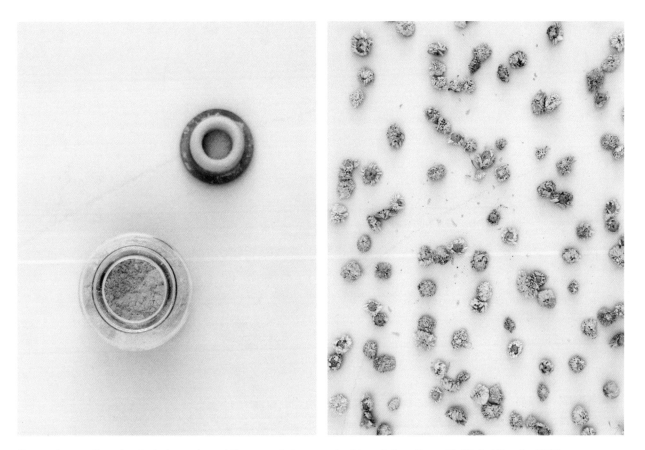

Dyers chamomile extracted pigments and flowers, diploma project in collaboration with Michel Garcia, 2016

When the colours appear in the pot,
it is quite magical and gives me the
feeling of being some kind of alchemist
or a witch. I find it incredible that plants
can have so many secrets.

An Introduction
to Bookbinding

Kathy Abbott

fig. 1

fig. 2

Bookbinding is an ancient craft practice with a long and culturally diverse tradition. It is a skilful craft with many processes and requires a good deal of patience, but the rewards are rich and the craft is hugely satisfying.

A bookbinder takes gatherings/sections of paper or parchment and sews them together to form a book-block. A cover is then made to protect the sewn pages; this can be made separately or as an integral part of the book's structure. The covers can be left unadorned or decorated and lettered in myriad ways. There are also many different book structures in which the book can be bound.

fig. 3
This Gospel, buried with St Cuthbert in 698, was recovered from his grave in 1104. Its beautiful red leather binding is original.

Bookbinding began as a way to protect and house written pages of text. The earliest bindings (in the codex form that we are most familiar with) date from around 200 CE and were created by the Coptic Christians of Egypt and Ethiopia. The Copts originally wrote on papyrus sheets with brushes and ink. They needed a way to keep these loose pages together so they started to sew the pages. Covers made of laminated papyrus, sometimes covered with leather, were then also sewn to the pages to protect them. The covers were often decorated with scribed lines and geometric shapes in the Islamic tradition. Because of its fragility, papyrus wasn't easy to fold so a different material was required. Parchment was widely used in the form of scrolls but it also had the bonus of being foldable and could be written upon on both sides. Parchment is a hygroscopic (moisture-absorbing) material and curls easily, so wood superseded the papyrus covers, as a way to keep the parchment weighted flat; sometimes clasps were added to aid this. The use of the codex book form spread widely and travelled via trade routes through the Islamic world and into Europe via Moorish Spain and Venice in Italy.

The earliest decorated English binding was discovered in the twelfth century, in the tomb of St Cuthbert who had been buried on the island of Lindisfarne, just off the north-east coast of England. St Cuthbert had died in 687, and the tiny book found with his body was a Gospel of St John, sewn in the Coptic tradition and protected by wooden boards covered with leather over raised gesso interlacing lines and a leaf ornament – the design being influenced by both Coptic and Western ornamental styles. This binding, together with a few others found from around this period, is very unusual, as surprisingly no other decorated English bindings exist from the following few centuries.

The earliest European book production was conducted solely by monks, who wrote, illustrated and bound all books until the early Middle Ages. Since book production was both laborious and highly skilled, books were expensive and accessible only to the clergy, royalty and the very wealthy. It wasn't until the invention of the European printing press in 1440 and the switch from the use of parchment to paper – which was much cheaper to produce – that books became more accessible to a wider audience and the need for bookbinders grew exponentially.

Books have always been decorated: from the earliest Coptic examples and the highly decorated bindings of the Islamic tradition to the richly jewelled bindings and the heavily blind-stamped covers of medieval times, to the gold-tooled examples of the following centuries. Nowadays, the decoration of bindings has become a way for contemporary bookbinders to express themselves creatively, usually in response to the text inside.

Today 'bookbinding' is a kind of umbrella term, used to describe all forms of book making: craft bookbinding, fine binding, design binding, box-making, trade binding, edition binding and commercial binding as well as book arts and artists' books and also book restoration and conservation.

fig. 4
Sewing frame.

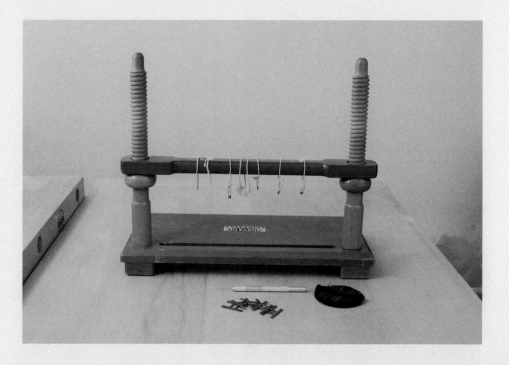

fig. 5

fig. 6

fig. 5
Gluing up the spine of a book, held in a finishing press, on the bench at the Wyvern Bindery, London.

fig. 6
Gold tooling using an engraved brass hand tool, commonly used for applying titles to book covers and spines at the Wyvern Bindery, London.

Historically, a bindery separated out each of the specialist tasks involved in the creation of a finished book: there would be a 'forwarding' department, which involved all the processes needed to make the pages into a book form, and then a 'finishing' department, where highly skilled bookbinders, or 'finishers', would decorate the bindings with gold leaf, jewels, onlays and inlays. Each bookbinder would have a role: folding the pages into sections, sewing the pages together, gilding or decorating the book's edges, shaping and lining the spine, and then covering the book-block. The completed book would then go to the 'finishing' department for decoration and lettering. In commercial binderies many of these tasks are now mechanised. Traditionally, one had to train as an apprentice for seven or eight years to become a bookbinder: the same length of time it takes to become a doctor!

The modern craft bookbinder generally works alone either at home or in a studio and makes books from scratch. The traditional bookbinding process begins with the folding and cutting of paper to form sections, which the binder then sews by hand, either on a bench or on a sewing frame. The result is the book-block. Endpapers are subsequently attached, either by sewing them or lightly gluing them to the book-block. The spine of the sewn book is glued and left square or shaped into a round (rounding) or into a round with shoulders, to accommodate the cover boards (rounding and backing).

fig. 7
Edge gilding using foil at the bindery of Barnard and Westwood.

The edges of the pages of the book can be coloured/decorated/gilded within a laying press – which clamps the pages tightly shut – so that no colour bleeds into the book-block. Decorative endbands (head and tail bands, either hand-sewn or ready-made), are attached to the spine, and then the spine is lined, usually with a fabric lining followed by paper.

The cover can be made separately from the book-block and joined to it later via the endpapers, or the cover boards can be first attached to the book-block and then the covering material formed over and around the boards. The materials used for covering the book's boards are generally leather (usually goatskin or calfskin prepared especially for bookbinding), vellum (parchment), fabric or specialist book-cloth, or paper.

To finish the book, the endpapers are pasted/glued and attached to the cover boards in either case. The covers can be left plain or decorated by way of lettering, tooling or decorating with gold leaf; foil blocking, inlays, onlays and so on. All of these traditional processes continue to be done by hand; there are not usually any mechanised processes involved in this type of bookbinding. It requires a lot of skill and patience to make a well-made book by hand.

Book artists utilise the book's form to make a work of art in book form. These may be small editions (created completely by the book artists themselves or in collaboration with printers/printmakers) or unique artworks.

Book conservators or restorers aim to stabilise or restore an existing bookbinding. It is imperative that the book conservator/restorer has had some training in bookbinding, so that they fully understand the 'mechanics' of each book they work on.

Bookbinding is still a very popular craft. There never seems to be a shortage of people wanting to learn this wonderful skill, but sadly there are no full-time college courses available in the UK, nor (at the time of writing) are there any apprenticeships on offer. Despite this seemingly gloomy situation, the future looks very bright for bookbinding: plenty of people are learning the craft via short and longer courses, in daytime, evening and weekend classes all over the country. Also, many people are now learning the craft via books, online courses and YouTube tutorials. Personally, I don't think there is a better way to learn bookbinding than via hands-on, face-to-face teaching, with a good tutor: problems can be quickly addressed and bad habits or techniques easily corrected.

Bookbinding is an immersive, meditative and mindful craft – and one that it is possible to do into a ripe old age!

Kathy Abbott served a four-year apprenticeship in bookbinding and then gained a Higher National Diploma from the London College of Printing, London (UK), followed by a BA (Hons) degree in Bookbinding from University of Roehampton, now London. She teaches advanced level Fine Binding at the City Lit, London, and conducts bookbinding workshops across the UK and overseas. She is a partner in Benchmark Bindery, established in 2009 with Tracey Rowledge, a founder member of the group Tomorrow's Past, and is the author of *Bookbinding: A step-by-step guide*, published by the Crowood Press in 2010. Read more about Kathy and her bookbinding work on pp. 92–95.

El Lanham

El Lanham (born in Essex, UK) is a multi-disciplinary artist whose work spans bookbinding, printmaking and tattooing. He grew up in Essex and studied Graphic Design at the University of the West of England Bristol, where he spent most of his time looking at books, making books, and trying to figure out what a book is and can be. After a stint working as a designer, he embarked on a two-year apprenticeship in hand bookbinding at the Royal Collection Trust – part of the Queen's Bindery Apprenticeship Scheme. It was during this training that he learned the traditional book-making skills he still uses in his practice today.

At age 24, Lanham moved his life and work to Lisbon, Portugal, to set up his studio where he has been since 2019. It is a third-floor atelier in Lisbon's historic centre – the building a survival from the 1st Marquis of Pombal's rebuilding of the city after the 1755 earthquake. The space was originally an apartment but it has been an artist studio for some time, with many emerging artists coming and going over the years. Lanham shares his space with the printmaking studio Lisboa Social Press and the tattoo studio THEY TATTOO, which he co-founded with the artist Thomas Langley. 'I feel so alive here. It's got a banging community of creatives and it's an inspiring place to be.'

His creative process is centred around storytelling and smile-making. As he says, the crafts that occupy him are 'just different ways to tell a story'. He is mostly led by the content of the book itself, meticulously researching each narrative, which eventually forms the foundation of his concepts. Sketches, writing and making numerous mock-ups are all part of his artistic approach. 'I make one-of-a-kind or small-run editions.

My work embraces the traditional and the contemporary. It's tactile and not too serious. Queer narratives play a big part in my work – I like to focus on making books from queer authors or projects that celebrate the queer narrative. I'm currently working on a print series "A Queer Pilgrimage" which celebrates LGBTQIA+ spaces,' he says.

Lanham sees his book making as partially a response to the digital age of mass production and throw-away culture. For him the book is a ritualistic object – a blend of function, information and art. 'I aim to make books that celebrate the book as an experience. I want to make

things that beg to be held, to be looked at, and I hope to make people question: What is a book? What value does it have? What does this book say to me?'

Lanham's work marries the traditional and contemporary. His practice is closely aligned with the slow making movement and uses traditional tools, even if the content itself explores more modern narratives. 'The simplicity of working with my hands is really what I love most about my creative practice, and seeing something that's not a book become a book,' he says. He enjoys experimenting with materials and tools, and is currently exploring tattooing leather. 'I can hear

Backing a small book in the press.

Sewing a textblock.

book conservators shuddering at this idea, but it's an interesting approach and I really love mixing techniques in this way to make something unexpected,' he adds.

He finds his ultimate inspiration hard to pinpoint. 'It's simultaneously everywhere and nowhere. It comes from fleeting moments, an endless curiosity, from collaborations, from wild experimentation, and often from queer narratives.' He finds himself looking to other disciplines and finding inspiration from unexpected fields, but he is also drawn to the work of the Dutch graphic designer Irma Boom and Visual Editions for breaking the barriers of 'the book'.

As for his evolution as an artist, Lanham is still discovering exactly where his path in book making will take him. He considers himself a generalist, rather than a specialist, and wants to continue experimenting with different techniques, materials and collaborating on more projects with queer authors, artists and practitioners.

Book inspired by the work of
Marlow Moss and Betty Parsons.

*Between Me and Life: A
Biography of Romaine Brooks.*

The simplicity of working with my hands is what I love most about my creative practice, and seeing something that's not a book become a book.

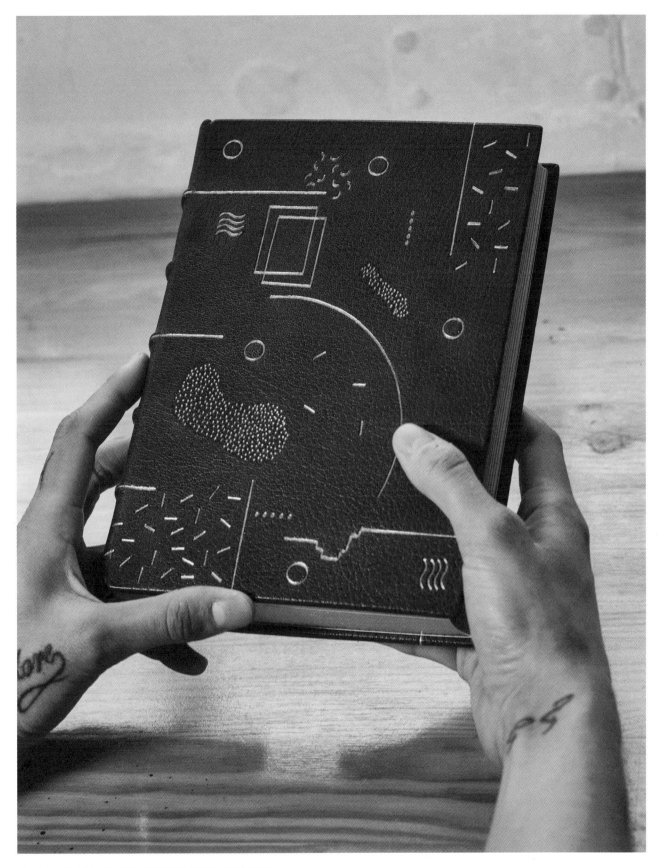

Book inspired by Derek Jarman's Prospect Cottage.

Morina Mongin

Born in Savannakhet in Laos, a city on the banks of the Mekong River, Morina Mongin arrived in France at just two years old with her parents who were welcomed as 'stateless' political refugees. She grew up in Besançon, the birthplace of Victor Hugo, before going to Paris for her studies.

Since then, she has lived and worked in Paris as a working bookbinder. She has an apartment near the place de l'Étoile and a studio in the heart of the Latin Quarter, on the rue de Navarre between the Arènes de Lutèce and the Jardin des Plantes, among the booksellers and writers. 'It is a square room on the ground floor in a 1930s building, overlooking a courtyard with trees where the light in the morning is very bright and warm. I work facing the window, on a piece of marble (my altar) placed on a paper cabinet,' she says. She describes her studio as a very intimate

space, like an echo chamber, where she sometimes spends sleepless nights finishing commissions.

Mongin says of her practice: 'Books have been and remain my lifeline ... I stay true to myself without trying to please, without submerging myself in any kind of trend, a group or a defined market. To say that I live through and for books is an under- statement. Novels or films that give a presence to binding, however small, touch me deep down to the core – as if, through this element, I was somehow involved in the plot.'

She feels a liturgical, even erotic relation- ship, with the act of bookbinding. Mongin is a creative binder, and her work, as she puts it, is 'the fruit of a slow gestation'. 'Like any form of sublimated sexuality, [bookbinding] is a crucible for alchemy.' For her, creative binding is more than a vocation; it is a calling that requires the commitment of body and spirit, 'that is to say, of the flesh'. 'I give everything of myself,' she says.

Mongin asks her writer friends to entrust her with their books, enriched with handwritten documents, photographs or drawings to provide the binding that will embody them. She seeks to accentuate the harmony between the time of the writing and the time of the binding.

She binds in the French style, according to a traditional technique: with full leather binding sewn on five cords, lined edge to edge, with suede goatskin flyleaves, stored in a folder and a leather-edged slip-case.

She has written a manifesto entitled *Relier aujourd'hui à la française* (French Bookbinding Today), where she explains her fascination with this form and its history.

Mongin has also developed a flexible binding technique in parchment stitched onto hair. It involves a 'dry' technique, which is to say that it does not use water-based glue. She prefers to work with vellum, which is made of calfskin that has been treated with lime. 'Its thinness and transparency make it a material close to human skin – at least from a phantasmagorical point of view – a material that doesn't even need to be scraped, which breathes and contracts like a living membrane and which, as a support for the written word,

To say that I live
through and for books
is an understatement.

becomes a surface to be painted, as one would visit a much-loved piece of skin with one's tongue.' She is incorporating more organic elements like fingernails, hair, eyelashes, saliva, bones, fat and blood, as well as other labile materials such as porcelain rings or casting wax, into her designs.

Her creative process starts with reading and examining the texts. She will undo the book's seam, prepare the ends of the sections, and trim the dust jacket. 'The

book will then be reassembled, sewn back together, rebuilt, constructed one stage at a time, month by month, faithfully following the technique and staying true to the movements that will stand the test of fatigue and contingencies,' she says.

She describes the process as 'a dance best performed in the morning on an empty stomach, in bare feet, with my hair tied back in a bun and the windows open.' She continues: 'I live with the text and its context. If the inspiration holds and it's a

painted binding, I am capable of spending a whole day breathing Dovanol while thinning my paraloïd with a size 0 brush!'

If she becomes stuck, she will keep on working until she has made the folder and slipcase and the cover, keeping the binding 'Jansenist', without decoration, until she can visualise the binding. 'When I'm in the shower, while peeling my vegetables, or when I'm talking about something else ... I won't let it go. For me, this is the highpoint, when the creative process moves out of the workshop and completely takes over the rest of my life.'

She considers that the binding is born several times: 'In the desire of the client who gives you carte blanche. In the response of the materials that give you back more than the sum of your gestures – a matrix for creativity. And in the finished binding, which becomes a kind of apparition and gets away from you, just as our own children remain a mystery and move on to live their own lives.'

Left: French boxcalf leather binding, photos printed on Japanese paper onlays, paraloïd paintings, 2020. *Phantom Thread*, Paul Thomas Anderson, original script of Vicky Krieps, 2016.

Middle: Miniature bone and vellum binding on a leporello letterpress printed by Michael Caine, 2020. *vulve amère ravive,* poem and three pop-ups by Morina Mongin, Paris, LRC, 2019, 1/12 copies of the first edition.

Right: French boxcalf leather binding, hairs and title onlays, 2019. *Belle de Jour*, Joseph Kessel, Paris, Gallimard, 1929, 1/100 copies on vélin pur fil Lafuma-Navarre, first edition.

Edge-to-edge doublure and suede goatskin flyleaves of a full boxcalf French binding, 2017. *Derrière son double*, Jean-Pierre Duprey, engraving by Jacques Hérold, Paris, Le Soleil Noir, 1950, 1/345 copies of the first edition.

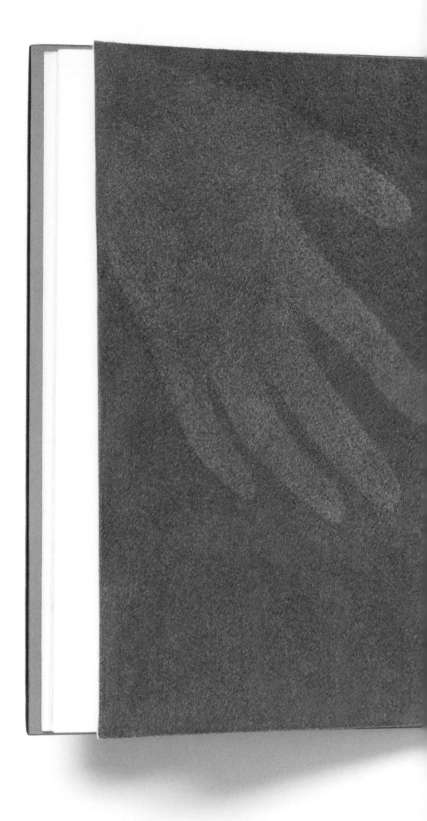

Mou111 Mou111 2O17

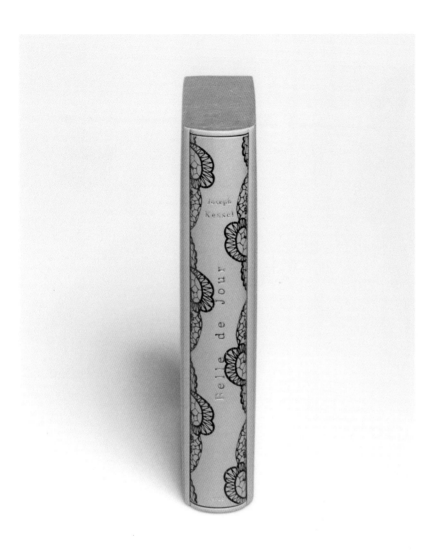

Stingray skin doublure, on a boxcalf french binding, 2019. *Belle de Jour*, Joseph Kessel, Paris, Gallimard, 1929, 1/100 copies on vélin pur fil Lafuma-Navarre, first edition.

Novels or films that give a presence to binding, however small, touch me deep down to the core – as if through this element, I was somehow involved in the plot.

Awagami Factory

The Awagami Factory is a world-renowned eighth-generation papermill operated by the Fujimori family in Tokushima, Shikoku, Japan. It has been making papers for over three hundred years, and the factory is able to handle all facets of paper-making. The factory has both handmade and machine-made washi papermaking sections, as well as hand-dyeing (including natural indigo) and stationery sections and a printmaking studio (traditional and digital). It supplies papers for a number of different creative markets including fine art and photography, interior design, publishing, art conservation, and print and packaging design.

In terms of traditional Japanese washi paper, *tamezuki* and *nagashizuki* are the two handmade methods that Awagami employs, with *tamezuki* being the older of the two. According to contemporary sources, the papermaking process in the Heian period (794–1185) proceeded as follows. First, plant fibres such as kōzo (mulberry), hemp, and gampi were cut into small pieces and heated in a mild alkaline solution. Next, the cooked material was rinsed, cleaned and beaten to break down the fibres. The resulting pulp was then mixed with water and scooped onto a screened frame. Prior to the water being drained away, the papermaker gently shook the frame, or 'mould', to even out the pulp distribution. Newly formed sheets of paper were stacked on top of each other, separated by cloth to prevent them from sticking together. Today, all Awagami washi papers are made using natural renewable fibres such as kōzo, bamboo, mitsumata, gampi and hemp.

Awagami has made washi paper, as well as custom-made washi papers, for many fine book editions. Throughout its long and illustrious history, the mill has worked

Awagami's Satomi-san forming a sheet of thick Tesuki-style washi.

Agitating the pulp.

Inspecting a custom-made sheet of washi –
looking for tiny kōzo bark flecks.

with publishers, bookbinders, artists' book makers, book conservators and even Buddhist temples. It strongly believes that, as a book is designed to be handled, paper plays a crucial part in its overall design and impact.

In the West, Awagami is perhaps best known for its fine art and photographic inkjet papers which have garnered attention thanks to collaborative projects with high-profile artists such as Frank Stella, Chuck Close and Richard Serra, among others. While these international artists are also recognised in Japan, in its home country Awagami is better known for its papers for interiors (shoji, fusuma and wallpapers) as well as those for printing and publishing; there is also a fast-growing interest in its inkjet washi.

Community is important to the mill and, out of the 43 staff, more than 35 live locally; many walk or bike to work. Awagami operates a paper museum and gallery space, and holds weekly paper art and craft workshops for the local community. The mill also hosts regular visits from many schoolchildren in the region, who come for a day of creative papermaking working alongside master papermakers.

The mill is always a hive of activity, including, but not limited to, hand and machine papermaking (from the harvesting, cleaning and beating of fibres to actual sheet formation), indigo dyeing, the making of stationery and interior artworks, creating custom papers for artists and publishers, and shipping orders to over 50 countries around the world. The mill also runs a visiting artists' programme and hosts international print shows.

Awagami often draws inspiration from the artisans themselves; they are always challenging themselves to develop new papers and related goods that are relevant for the modern day. International artists and designers both inspire and push them to stay relevant in a fast-changing and hyper-competitive world.

While Awagami has adapted its business to satisfy advances in technology, craft remains at the core of everything it does. Its craftspeople still practise a wide range of traditional crafts including not only hand papermaking but also indigo dyeing, orizome (paper dyeing and folding) and Japanese-style bookbinding. Workers consider themselves first and foremost as craftspeople, and they consider that everything they do is based on craft knowledge handed down to them over hundreds of years.

The proudest achievements for the mill have been the many members of the family who have been honoured as 'Cultural Treasures of Japan' by the emperor, as well as commissions to create special washi papers for imperial ceremonies and sacred Buddhist books.

Bamboo washi pads dry under pressure.

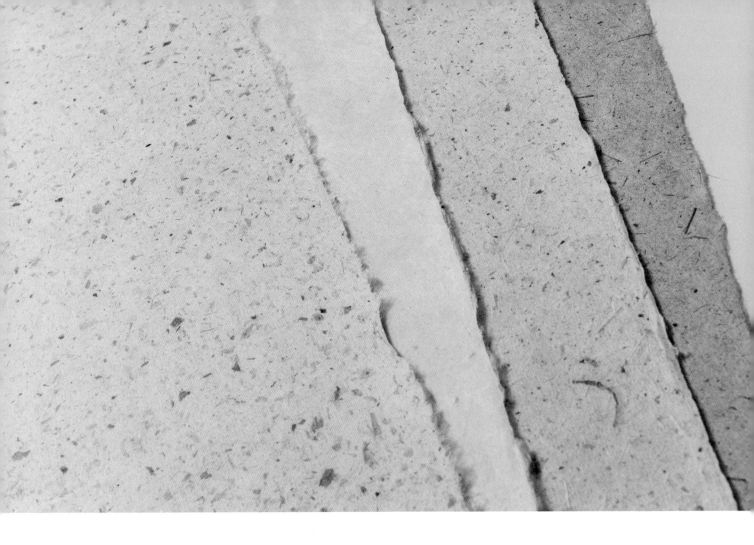

Above: Awagami 'Nature Paper' collection made with local agricultural waste (onion, melon, radish, etc.). **Left:** Handmade 'Shikishi' paper with indigo and gold leaf – typically used for calligraphic works.

AWAGAMI FACTORY

Awagami hand-dyed indigo 'Wacho' notebook.

Today, all our washi papers are still made using natural renewable fibres such as kōzo, bamboo, mitsumata, gampi and hemp.

Tracey Rowledge

Born in Kingston, UK, and having studied both Fine Bookbinding and Conservation at Guildford College of Further and Higher Education, and Fine Art at Goldsmiths, University of London, the artist Tracey Rowledge's practice has evolved in a way that combines both her fine art and craft training. 'My work is ideas based as opposed to being discipline-specific. I enjoy the fluidity I have to enjoy the space in between,' she says.

Working out of her studio in west London that she shares with friend and fellow artist Kathy Abbott (see p. 92), her practice encompasses fine binding, book arts and book conservation. Rowledge draws on this breadth of knowledge when navigating how best to respond to any book that she binds.

As her work is not fixed to a particular discipline, she often finds it hard to describe, saying, 'A new piece of work will take me in a particular direction, although the impulse for the majority of my work is to explore gestural mark-making through different craft processes, to create a play between how an image looks on the surface and how it was actually made, and to juxtapose process with the appearance of spontaneity.' She allows the book to guide her decision making, only ever doing what feels right for the book. She doesn't consider herself to have a speciality, although gold tooling is what she is best known for.

Her ambition with each project is to make an object that not only functions well but with which people can connect on a number of levels. That might be an aesthetic or emotional connection; one that could change over time as the book is reread and new understandings and connections are established.

Rowledge's creative process always begins with thinking. 'I love the rigorous process of thinking and how developing an idea and transforming it into a piece of work can enable me to see the world from a different perspective,' she explains. She is inspired by creating a functional object and in a lot of cases a functional *art* object, 'Each book takes you on a different journey, and it's often the most challenging books I bind that result in the most creative responses.'

Depending on the original idea, she could end up with a drawing, a sculpture or a book. If the starting point is a printed text-block, then she will begin by getting to know the text and the physicality of the

The Odyssey of Homer
and *The Battle of
The Frogs and Mice,*
Homer (translated by
Alexander Pope), 1807.
A Tomorrow's Past
conservation binding.
The textblock is laced
onto a double wrapper
structure, using a series
of folds and turn-ins
that double back
on themselves. The
wrapper structure
is made from hand-
coloured handmade
paper with fore-edge
ties. Bound in 2011.

Each book takes you on a different journey, and it's often the most challenging books I bind that result in the most creative responses.

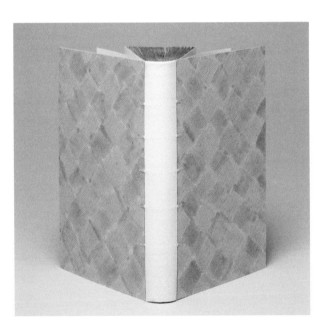

Select Fables of Esop and Other Fabulists, R. Dodsley, c. 1788.
A Tomorrow's Past conservation binding, bound with a handmade paper inner wrapper and handcoloured boards laced on with linen tapes. Bound in 2013.

Fables by the Late Mr Gay, London, 1823.
A Tomorrow's Past conservation binding, bound using the original boards and covered in handmade paper, stencilled with acrylic to reflect the oval motif running through the book. Bound in 2017.

text-block and respond to this through the imagery she creates for the cover and endpapers. It will also inform the colours she chooses to work with. 'I'll then draw on my bookbinding, book conservation and book arts knowledge to best respond to meet the physical needs of the text-block,' says Rowledge. She will also utilise the structure of the book to draw another parallel to the text, but in a more subtle way, so that the book handles in a very particular way. First developing the structure through a series of maquettes, she will make her technical and creative decisions. At that point, Rowledge will begin binding or rebinding the book, which once completed is housed in a cloth-covered drop-back box.

She especially enjoys working collaboratively with other makers and considers this a highlight of her career. Another memorable high point was an extraordinary Arctic expedition to western Greenland with the artist-led environmental charity Cape Farewell, for which she was funded by the UK's Crafts Council. A formative moment in the development of her practice as a mid-career maker, the trip was organised to raise awareness about the climate crisis. She returned with a whole new body of work, leaving the ship with three suites of drawings. She reflects on the trip saying, 'It took me a long time to assimilate this experience and the work I'd made. It was such an intense experience, enabling me to reconnect with working more intuitively again. It was a key moment in my career.'

Hoppus's Practical Measurer, 1848. A Tomorrow's Past conservation binding, The structure forms the cover and spine lining in one. Covered in handmade paper, with a coloured pencil drawing across cover. Bound in 2019.

James Cropper Mill & The Paper Foundation

A view over Burneside and the James Cropper Mill.

Mark Cropper (born in Kendal, UK) is chair of his family business, James Cropper, active as master papermakers since 1845. He grew up in Burneside on the edge of the English Lake District. After studying English Literature at Edinburgh University, he embarked on a career in renewable energy, before setting up a small hydro-electric development business. He eventually moved back to the Lake District with his family, joining the board of his family business in 2006 and becoming chair in 2010. 'I live in the same house and have the same profession as generations of my family – an extraordinary privilege,' he says.

The family business runs two papermills. The first dates back to 1746 and is highly specialised, making everything from packaging for luxury brands to the carbon-fibre paper used in the production of green hydrogen. This mill is both ancient and modern. Nearly 100 people work in innovation and are always coming up with new ideas, particularly processes and products that are more sustainable. Their latest venture is Colourform, a high-quality moulded pulp packaging available in a wide variety of colours and textures. It is now replacing plastics in premium spirits and cosmetics.

The second mill, opened in 2015, is Cropper's personal project, set up with the goal of revitalising and celebrating the UK's papermaking heritage and building stronger links with the local community. The Paper Foundation is a charity focused on preserving the critically endangered craft of making paper by hand. The charity has been salvaging historical papermaking tools for a few years now, and this led to them to set up a new paper manufactory in 2020. 'It's in an old cowshed at the back of my house!' Cropper says. 'There's only two of us involved so far, but we have great hopes it will grow. We've saved about 800 papermaking moulds, some of which are 250 years old, so there's plenty to make use of.'

Mark Cropper in the mill.

Paper artefacts of any kind relied on handmade paper until the 1800s and we believe the preservation of this trade and associated arts is incredibly important.

Separating sheets of dried paper in the Paper Foundation.

Pulling a sheet of paper from the vat.

Emptying the vat.

Community is vital to the mill's future, and vice versa. 'Our community is ultimately what sustains us, and if it is not sustainable then we won't be either. Providing education, jobs, workspaces and housing for younger people has to be a priority as these are poorly provided for at the moment,' Cropper says.

Both mills are critical to book making and related crafts, both in the UK and farther afield. James Cropper has made the Wibalin book-cloth range for Winter & Co. (used on the large majority of conventional hardback books) since the late 1970s, and has been making Colorplan and other ranges for G.F. Smith for even longer. The Paper Foundation is now the

only producer of handmade papers for the repair and conservation of books. Cropper comments: 'Paper artefacts of any kind relied on handmade paper until the 1800s, and we believe the preservation of this trade and associated arts is incredibly important. There's also a huge amount of lost knowledge to rediscover in the world of handmade paper, from how raw materials are prepared and used to the way paper was finished ... We are worried that many aspects of the art of the book are being squeezed and want to address it in a small local way if we can.' His foundation is beginning this journey of rediscovery. It will have an archive and library, and the plan is to create a bindery, print and decorative paper studio as well

Historical moulds and deckles for hand papermaking. Some of the antique moulds in the collection at the Foundation date back to 1800.

as a paper conservation centre. Cropper is especially excited by the prospect of exploring the lost art of Renaissance and medieval papermaking.

Cropper's favourite paper stocks are the company's handmade paper range that pushes the boundaries of texture and feel in a way that Cropper believes is only possible when making paper by hand. Japanese papers and bindings – and indeed Japan's deep appreciation of paper and its innate artfulness – are the things Cropper reveres the most. 'The standout object for me is a nineteenth-century Japanese sample book of pinpricked indigo patterns. The book itself is a treasure with a deeply em-bossed cover and gold-leaf-decorated endpapers, but the 216 patterns inside, each labelled and carefully pasted, six to each page, are beyond description. They are staggeringly beautiful and unlike anything else I have ever seen.'

Finished paper on the packing bench in the mill.

An Introduction to Papermaking

Tom Frith-Powell

The author takes
a paper mould
from the shelf.

Paper was invented approximately two thousand years ago in China. According to a story circulating in the fourth century AD, Cai Lun, a eunuch at the Chinese imperial court, made the first paper from the bark of trees mixed with old rags and hempen fishing nets and successfully used it as a writing surface, thereby pleasing the emperor immensely. Archaeological evidence suggests that, in fact, paper had existed for some centuries before Cai Lun, and the circumstances surrounding the invention of paper remain obscure. Regardless, knowledge of how to make paper had spread from China to neighbouring countries including Japan, Korea and India by as early as the third century AD. Chinese missionaries keen to share Buddhist scholarship and religion were taught to make paper, brushes and ink in order to aid the dissemination of their message.

By 751 AD paper had arrived in Samarkand, then the centre of the Islamic world, from where it spread across that world. It was not until the eleventh century, over a thousand years after its invention, that paper first arrived in Europe. It was the Muslim rulers of southern Spain who established the continent's first papermills. The emergence of administrative government and bureaucracy in Europe led to the export of paper from Spain to Italy, France and Germany as an economical alternative to parchment, which was made from animal skins. By the late thirteenth century the first papermills had been established in northern Italy. At this time, monks were still painstakingly copying out manuscripts onto expensive parchment, and paper was used primarily in commercial dealings. It wasn't until the mid-fifteenth century when Johannes Gutenberg invented moveable type and a semi-mechanised printing press that papermaking in Europe really took off.

Gutenberg's innovation allowed books to be mass-produced for the first time, and in so doing he invented the book as it exists today. The success of printing as a technology relied upon the prior existence, and ready availability, of paper. Without it, printing would not have been a commercial success. Gutenberg's Bible, printed in 1455, was an edition of around 200. Of those, approximately thirty-five were printed on parchment made from calf skin, of which twelve survive, while the remainder were printed on handmade paper, of which thirty-six survive. Simple economics demanded that the printers offset the high costs of casting the type and manning the press by printing in large editions. By printing on paper instead of vellum, it was possible to bring books to market at an affordable price. In the years succeeding Gutenberg's Bible, a printing revolution spread across Europe which needed paper in quantities never seen before.

In order to satisfy the surge in demand for laboriously hand-made paper, linen and hempen rags had to be collected, sorted and prepared. The ragman played an important role in European society for centuries, until a scarcity of rags precipitated the development of new papers made from wood bast in the mid-nineteenth century. The ragman roamed the land gathering discarded textiles, bedlinen, sails, rigging, ropes and clothing, before selling them on to papermills, where they were processed for papermaking.

Upon arriving at the mill, the rags were sorted and chopped before undergoing a process of fermentation called retting that softened them, making them susceptible to pulverisation in water. This is the 'beating' process, during which the fermented rags are stamped and beaten by large wooden hammers until the desired consistency is reached. Added to water, the result is a milky-looking solution, its whiteness an effect of the plant fibres suspended in the water.

figs. 1–6: Plates from Denis Diderot and Jean le Rond d'Alembert, *Encyclopédie* – 'Papeterie', *Supplément à l'Encyclopédie ou Dictionnaire raisonné des sciences, des arts et des métiers,* vol. 5 (Paris, 1765).

fig. 1

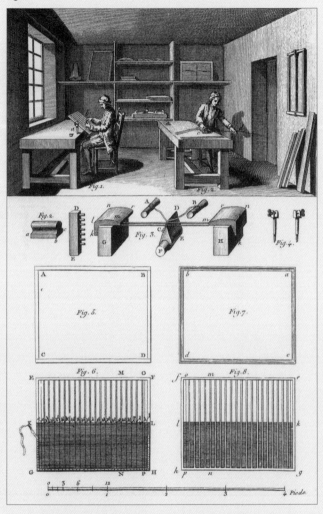

fig. 2

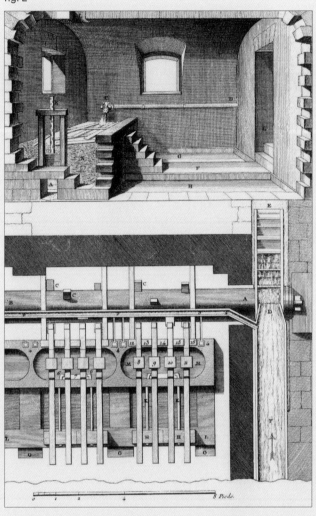

Mould making: This plate shows a paper mould in the process of being made. A paper mould is a wooden frame with wire mesh on which the sheets of paper are formed.

Retting: In the days when all paper was made from rags, the rags were first retted. This was a process of fermentation which softened the rags and started the process of breaking up the fibres.

fig. 3

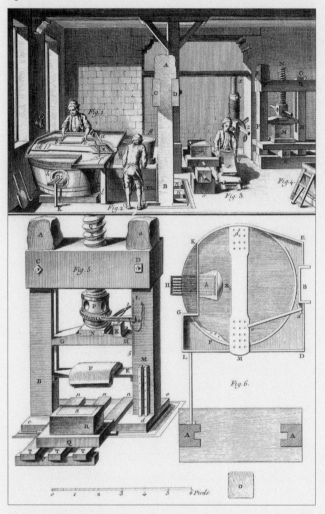

fig. 4

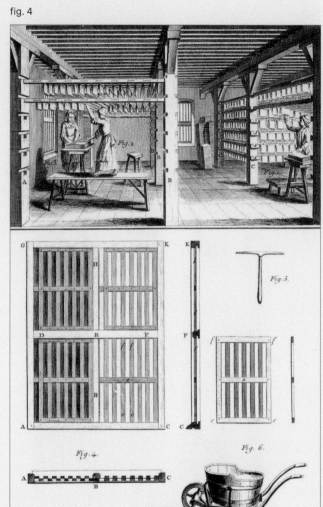

Sheet formation: A papermaker dips a mould into a vat filled with paper pulp (a mixture of fibre and water) before pulling it out to form a sheet of paper.

Drying: After pressing, the paper is hung from ropes in the drying loft.

fig. 5

fig. 6

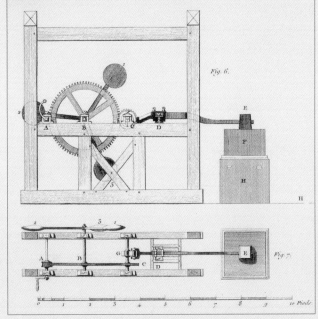

Sizing: Once dry, the paper is dipped into a bath of gelatine solution. This 'sizes' the paper, making it less absorbent to water; otherwise it would be like blotting paper.

Sorting: Before being sent out to customers, the sheets of paper are sorted into different grades: 'perfect' sheets with no imperfections and others with creases, smudges and other imperfections.

AN INTRODUCTION TO PAPERMAKING

To form a sheet, the vatman passes a papermaking mould through the water in the vat, giving it a careful shake as he lifts it out to ensure a uniform distribution across its surface. Writing in the sixteenth century, the German alchemist Michael Meier saw the moment of sheet formation as almost miraculous, during which the sheet rises 'like a phoenix out of her own ashes'. Each sheet is then transferred to a rectangle of dampened woollen felt slightly larger than the sheet by pressing the face of the mould (upon which the newly formed sheet now sits) onto the felt in a single rolling movement. Once this process has been repeated and a 'post' – or stack of fifty sheets interleaved between felts – built up, the sheet is transferred to the press for the first time. After an initial pressing between felts during which most of the water is expelled from the sheet, the now-damp sheets are peeled from the felts and laid on top of each other in a pack. This pack of sheets is pressed a number more times. Between each subsequent pressing the sheets are separated and again laid on top of each other in a different order. The more times this step is undertaken, the smoother the final sheet will be. After their final pressing the sheets are hung from drying racks until completely dry. Once dry, the sheets are stacked and stored under gentle pressure to flatten and 'cure'. While the paper will continue to improve with age, after three months it is sufficiently flat and has achieved its desired crispness.

While the process of making paper by hand has changed very little over the last thousand years, many technological advances have been made, the most significant of which was the invention of a new type of beater in the Netherlands in the late seventeenth century. This machine sped up the process of transforming rags into pulp. Despite this, it still takes three months to make a good sheet of paper. As late as the 1940s, the famous British paper-making company Whatman would not let a sheet leave its mill until it was at least six months old. From the mid-eighteenth century, papermaking, like many industrial processes, was transformed by a number of new inventions and discoveries.

In 1798 Nicholas-Louis Robert, a former French soldier who had spent time working a papermill in France, submitted a patent for a machine that produced paper in a continuous roll. Robert had to give up his patent, and the machine was ultimately developed by Henry and Sealey Fourdrinier in London, brothers whose name the machine bears to this day. Shortly after, in 1800, chemists discovered the chemical compound of cellulose, which ultimately made it possible to extract cellulose from wood, making trees an abundant source of papermaking fibre for the first time. These two developments laid the groundwork for the mechanised mass production of low-quality but cheap paper that persists to the present day.

With the emergence of a mass-produced, cheap and homogeneous product in the nineteenth century, the place of handmade paper changed. Whereas previously all paper had been handmade, once manufactured paper became widely available, handmade paper was reserved for use when paper of the highest quality and greatest beauty was required. In 1931 Whatman was proclaiming that 'in this age of mass production, the making of handmade paper remains as flourishing an industry as ever', sustained by those 'who see the value of the little extra which makes the thing done both durable and beautiful'.

This remains true today. High-quality handmade paper continues to be prized and sought after by many artists, designers, bookbinders and conservators, for whom handmade paper remains quite simply the best paper for their work. The industry, however, is no longer thriving. There are now only a handful of professional hand papermakers worldwide, and in the UK there are only two: the Paper Foundation, which specialises in the production of archival book, conservation and printing papers, and Two Rivers, which makes watercolour paper.

Tom Frith-Powell is the director and papermaker at the Paper Foundation. The Paper Foundation is a charity committed to ensuring the survival of papermaking by hand, the production of fine handmade paper and the celebration of paper and related arts, crafts and industries. Based in Burneside in the English Lake District, the Paper Foundation supplies fine handmade papers to the world's leading bookbinders, conservators, artists and designers. Prior to joining the Paper Foundation in early 2020, Tom worked in London for the artist Damien Hirst and at an architectural consultancy. He graduated from University College London in 2018.

WOMEN - ART - BELIEF

Women of all faiths and beliefs – religious and non-religious – are creating ground-breaking artistic work across west Yorkshire. At a time of heightened religious and racial discrimination, where women's identies, beliefs and religious practices are distorted through the lens of inflammatory media and political rhetoric, it is time to turn the spotlight to women artists, whose creative practices articulate the complexity of identity and belief. In this collection of postcards, twelve artists in West Yorkshire speak in their own words about how their work connects with, and is shaped by, their beliefs and identities.

Women - Art - Belief is a multi-arts project bringing together oral histories by Nabeelah Hafeez, portrait photography by Shanaz Gulzar and films by Paresh Solanki and Wahida Shaffi. Edited by Wahida Shaffi and Fiona Ranford.

Thank you for your
beautiful work Rose
:)
love Fiona
X

COMMUNITY

Rabbits Road Press

One of My Kind (OOMK) – a collaborative publishing practice – is the brainchild of Sofia Niazi, Rose Nordin and Sabba Khan, based in the central London borough of Newham, in the Somerset House Studios. Heiba Lamara joined the studio in 2014.

It began life as a zine that explored the art, faith and activism of women. Nordin, Niazi and Lamara often explored diverse subjects, such as fabric, print and the Internet, through the lens of Muslim women artists like themselves – something they felt unable to do within mainstream media. The zine also included contributions from non-Muslims, since they wanted it to create an honest reflection of their world.

Their printing studio, Rabbits Road Press (RRP), based on the ground floor of an old redbrick library in Newham, was launched in 2017 with just one RISO machine.

Several years later, they have three active machines, allowing them to take control of the means of production and open the studio up to others. Lamara explains, 'In calling ourselves a community-focused press we aim to cultivate a print community within the space; connect and work with schools, groups and institutions locally, and focus on education over commercial projects.'

RRP has become a lifeline for people to maintain a creative practice on a budget. The press welcomes art students, graduates who can no longer access art facilities, people who can't afford to attend art school, people looking for something to do on a Wednesday, people who grew up in Newham and have always wanted a local creative hub, people escaping their day jobs, zine-makers with a table at an upcoming fair, and people who have never made a zine before.

Heiba Lamara, Rose Nordin and Sofia Niazi at Rabbits Road Press.

As a format to create work in, we love that there are so many rules built into the book. It instantly creates parameters and forces us to rein in ideas.

OOMK hasn't stopped there. Over the past decade, the trio has organised or co-organised many publishing fairs including DIY Cultures (London), Process (London) and Duplicate (Birmingham), and partici-pated both nationally and internationally in the wider self-publishing scene.

When considering the purpose of OOMK, Niazi cites the Trinidadian and Tobagonian activist, writer and publisher John La Rose, who spoke, she says, of 'publishing as a vehicle which gave an independent validation of one's own culture, history, politics – a sense of one's self'. She continues: 'That's certainly something we've found to be true. In quite an individualistic art world, we found publishing to be a friendly, collaborative and nurturing space to develop ideas, friendships and steer conversations in a way that we would never have been able to through mainstream media or through becoming a "big deal" artist.'

In relation to the collective's practice in the wider culture of book art, Nordin, Niazi and Lamara recognise that for a long time they have worked within their own unique ecosystem. However, due to their processes for making and organis-ing, which have been drawn from the DIY scene, they have always had a readiness to take on all aspects of making books, and through collaboration their participa-tion in the culture of books has evolved.

'As a format to create work in, I love that there are so many rules built into the book. It instantly creates parameters and forces us to rein in ideas. There is also ample room to break and bend the rules, and the book can be a very affordable and achievable medium to work in,' Niazi affirms.

At OOMK, the creative process between the three artists is always a collabora-tive one. They decide on a theme in an organic way – usually settling on what-ever speaks to them, on shared and current interests, and on what feels natural and obvious. They then host a 'think-in' open invitation to new contribu-tors to begin a conversation and develop ideas. They are inspired by other self-organised collectives and artists that work in print and crafts, such as See Red Women's Workshop, Sister Corita Kent and Faith Ringgold. Working outside the conventional parameters of art, they are more likely to be influenced by reading or conversation than visual references.

On their craft, Niazi concludes: 'I love making things by hand; I can't think in the same way with a computer screen. I find the process of making a lot more enjoy-able and collaborative when there are physical materials involved ... In a world that is so increasingly artificial, I appreci-ate art materials being physical and there being an element of unmediated surprise.'

Someone flicking through DIY Cultures Programme, which is co-curated by OOMK.

Rabbits Road Press launch pack.

Heiba Lamara.

In quite an individualistic art world, we found publishing to be a friendly, collaborative and nurturing space to develop ideas, friendships and steer conversations.

Tenderbooks

Tamsin Clark (born in Gloucester, UK) was introduced to the world of book art from a young age. She grew up in a small country town in Gloucestershire where her parents ran a gallery and produced small handmade publications from an Adana letterpress printer on their kitchen table. 'It was a childhood surrounded by artists and books,' she says.

In 2002 Clark moved her life to London to study American literature. She went on to work at Studio Voltaire, the Victoria and Albert Museum, and the Barbican Centre. She also ran an occasional project space from her flat in south London. She was always interested in DIY publishing and art taking place outside of a commercial or established gallery context. In 2012 she started making books with her friend Richard Bevan under the name Setsuko. 'Making publications has always been a fun endeavour first and foremost for me,

and I never thought that books would become my job! It all happened by luck and accident in a way,' she says. The books are almost entirely composed of images found during long periods of research. Clark is interested in how carefully sequenced images tell stories.

In comparison to working in a professional gallery context, she found the small-scale and immediate transaction of selling artists' books refreshing. 'I had always loved visiting Printed Matter in New York and Yvon Lambert in Paris, but although there are many interesting publishing projects happening in the UK, there seemed to be no established place to go for it,' Clark explains. So, in 2014, she opened Tenderbooks located in Cecil Court, a street with Victorian shop facades right at the heart of London's West End in between Soho and Covent Garden.

T.S. Eliot and Mozart lived here, and
Aleister Crowley and Graham Greene
were regular visitors to the bookshops.
It's a situation that still feels a little
radical to me.

With Tenderbooks, an aim is to make a space for experimental publishing in the middle of the city that could be open to not just an art crowd but also a more general audience. The shop can be many things: a distributor for a broad range of material, a publisher and facilitator for new work, and as a space that produces events and exhibitions. They also have a window display that acts as a miniature gallery that you can view when the shop is closed.

The shop occupies a space on a street full of independent businesses: shops selling antiques, rare maps and art as well as books. 'It's a special spot with a rich history. T.S. Eliot and Mozart lived here, and Aleister Crowley and Graham Greene were regular visitors to the bookshops. Despite being right in the heart of the city, it's a situation that still feels a little radical to me,' Clark says.

Tenderbooks is always busy hosting events for artists and bookmakers. While working in galleries, Clark would often get frustrated with how much planning was involved in realising events and exhibitions. 'In contrast, it feels like there can be such a refreshing "live-ness" about the publishing scene. All you have to do is buy some beer and put books on a table and you have an event to share with your friends. I love the feeling that our shop can respond quite immediately to what is being made right now,' she says.

Her motivation for running the shop is often renewed by the range of people who come through the door and the conversations she has with them.

Dieter Roth, *Gesammelte Werke band 1*, Edition Hansjörg Mayer, 1976.

John Bock, *The Maltreated Frigate* I–IV, Bornemisza
Art Contemporary and Walther König, 2006.

*Neko manma 'The Cat is Beautiful'
Photobook*, Shinko Music Publishing, 1985.

Providing an engaging space to browse in is something she feels proud of. 'With a small shop there's an atmosphere of sharing information that you can't get elsewhere. It's great showing people things, and customers recommend books to me all the time. It's reciprocal,' she says.

Tenderbooks has seen some beautiful rare books over the years, and Clark always feels sad to part with them; not necessarily the most valuable items but more one-of-a-kind things. The shop recently had a small collection of Japanese cinema ephemera including some striking examples of modernist design that it was a pleasure spending a bit of time with. The shop was also very proud to host a book display and publish a bookplate edition with artist AA Bronson.

An installation made by Cory Arcangel in the front window in the style of a real-estate window display with LED screens was one of her favourite exhibitions to date. Other notable events included exhibiting a complete run of the British experimental sound journal *MUSICS* curated by Thurston Moore, and a collaboration on the exhibition for the Most Beautiful Swiss Books Prize. Last year, Tenderbooks hosted an installation by architect Takeshi Hayatsu where the prize-winning books were displayed on giant stacks of paper.

When describing why she finds books so unique, Clark says that it's 'the idea of a whole world you can carry about in your pocket'.

Behind the Books – An Exhibition of the Most Beautiful Swiss Books, installation by Takeshi Hayatsu at Tenderbooks, 2020.

In contrast [to galleries], it feels like there can be such a refreshing 'liveness' about the publishing scene. All you have to do is buy some beer and put books on a table and you have an event to share with your friends.

Behind the Books – An Exhibition of the Most Beautiful Swiss Books,
installation by Sanchez Benton architects at Tenderbooks, 2019.

Utrecht

Utrecht is a bookshop and exhibition space in Jingumae, Shibuya-ku, Tokyo. It showcases a large collection of art publications from all over the world, most of them from independent publishers. It began life as an online shop in 2002, but when the team was unable to find bookshops selling books they would like to have, they opened a shop of their own. The shop is now run by Utrecht's director, Shie Okabe, manager Futoshi Miyagi and bookseller Teruki Ishii.

The Shibuya shop mainly deals with art, design and fashion-related books that are rarely seen in general bookstores. It sells unique, independent and small-run books made by writers and artists, especially those with unusual designs. Utrecht strives to create displays that highlight each book individually as well as the relationships between the books that sit side by side on the shelves. It's a place where customers can browse, pick up the books, and gradually evolve their own connection with them.

Utrecht also distributes its own publications and books, directly with domestic and overseas publishers, domestic art bookstores, and select shops. In addition, Utrecht is engaged in various book-related activities such as book selection at interior design and apparel shops, book curation at various facilities such as shared offices, and co-hosting of the Tokyo Art Book Fair, where it has a place on the committee.

When describing the enjoyment she takes from running a bookshop, Okabe says: 'The shop is at the core of our activity. We can meet new people, we can experience new things.' It is in this way that projects often happen by chance at Utrecht. Everyday occurrences can often lead to the start of a collaboration: 'For example, I bump into an artist and have a rambling conversation. Nice things take form from everyday, trivial matters.' Utrecht occasionally makes original items with artists that fit the shop's identity.

Entrance and installation view, *Kaoru Yokoo 'Book Echo'*, 2020.

The shop is at the core of our activity. We can meet new people, we can experience new things. Like when I bump into an artist and have a rambling conversation. Nice things take form from everyday, trivial matters.

Installation view, *Shin Hamada 'A Rock, a Paper, a Wind'*, 2020.

View of Xtra Small Book Fair, 2018.

They also make books in conjunction with exhibitions and have hosted many at the shop. Okabe recalls: 'There are many exhibitions we have had with artists and designers we admire ... Recently, we had an exhibition by Masayoshi Nakajo, one of the best designers in Japan. I was happy to meet him in person.'

The selection of the shop's stock happens at the weekly staff meeting. If a member of the team wants to sell a new book, then they must promote it in their own language. Utrecht wants to be a shop that can offer opportunities for book makers and readers alike. 'I always ask, "Would I want to have it?",' Okabe says.

She also stays true to some advice she was once given: 'You cannot encounter a good book unless we let go of the books we sell.' This, coupled with her past experience working for a company selling fly-fishing gear, maintains her 'catch-and-release faith', as she puts it.

When reflecting on any books she has had a hard time letting go of, she admits, 'There are simply too many to choose from.'

Ken Kagami's special box edition *Charr*, published by Utrecht, 2019, among Kagami's other books.

Sign made of resin, with Chinese character 'book' made with bones inside.

Granby Press

Sumuyya Khader (born in Liverpool, UK) runs Granby Press, a community-led print club and Risograph studio in Liverpool. It offers a new space for local creatives to experiment, socialise and make their art in an affordable and accessible way. Currently, it is just Khader running the press. 'We're in the listening phase – printing small runs for local galleries and artists, and showing people what's possible,' she says.

Khader describes herself as both an artist and an illustrator, but would prefer not to be defined by these labels. 'I studied fine art but have realised that there's a lot of joy and potential in not being put into an "artist" box,' she says.

Her work is very reactive and colourful, with the emphasis on illustration that focuses on exploring identity and place. 'Figures are really important, so their forms appear frequently. With my print-based work I'm always trying to convey a message or visually communicate and engage in a conversation,' she explains. In her work, she is hugely inspired by black culture, specifically in Liverpool but also further afield, that pushes boundaries. 'Watching other people take risks always inspires me to do the same,' Khader says.

The mission of the Granby Press is to print and share works by local people. Members of the community can use it as a base to come together and engage with each other through their art. The press offers Granby's ethnically diverse neighbourhood an opportunity to share their own unique stories. Khader wants to

Frank Ocean.

Bridge.

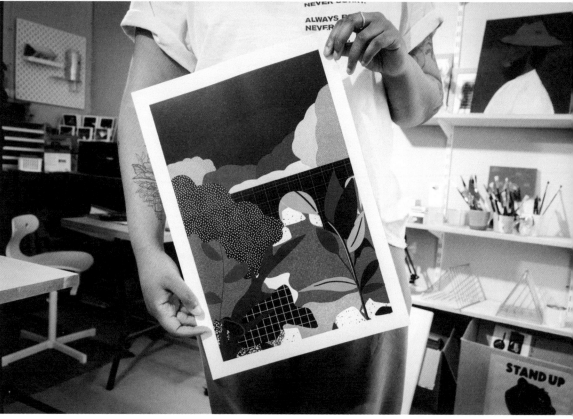

encourage local creatives to test out their ideas, and empower them to experiment.

'For me, it's about giving people a way of expressing themselves and being able to communicate without barriers. I think that's the true power of having an independent press – whether it's visually or via text, or a combination of these, you can author it as a community, an individual, a collective, or be anonymous, but directly speak to your community,' Khader explains.

Khader finds the world of self-publishing and zines a fascinating one. She believes being able to share your work is something that should be more widely available, and hopes that over time the Granby Press can facilitate the sharing of information through the use of print. 'The idea that someone living round the corner from the press has a short anthology or collection they want to share locally, but are unable to get it out there in the traditional sense due to barriers, is crazy,' she says.

The reaction and engagement the press will receive from the creative community in the local area is still unknown, since Khader is juggling running the press between a day job and freelance work. However, her first aim will be to share more about what Risograph printing is. She describes the future for the space: 'We will have examples available and an open door for people who are curious about the medium, so eventually it can be a true resource for the community.'

Selection of drawings and prints.

With my print-based work I'm always trying to convey a message and engage in a conversation.

I'm Black and I'm Proud, Risograph print.

Colorama

Johanna Maierski (born in Darmstadt, Germany) moved to Berlin as a child and never left. It's where she studied for an MA in Architecture and Urban Research, and where she now runs her studio. A publisher, teacher and printer, she established a small art press and RISO printing studio, Colorama, in 2015, based in the ACUD Kunsthaus in Berlin-Mitte. Since then she has exhibited and taught internationally, with Colorama's publications sold at book fairs and bookstores across the globe. Five years after opening the studio, together with Lauria Joan, she founded COLORAMA WORKSHOP, an educational community space for printing and book making at the Haus der Statistik in Berlin. Since 2016, together with Aisha Franz, Maierski has been hosting CLUBHOUSE, a yearly comic residency programme in Berlin.

Silk scarf with an illustration by Melek Zertal for a fashion project launched in conjunction with Zertal's publication *Together*.

Testprinting for SAP by Jul Quanouai.

As a book maker, printer and designer, Maierski is entirely self-taught. 'For the first six months as a printer, I didn't even know that paper had a grain direction. Since I didn't know anything about making books, my learning curve has been quite steep,' she recalls.

She credits her fellow printers with teaching her all she now knows, but also the bookbinder that she has been working with for some years now. Maierski's book making and designing have largely been shaped by the time she has spent at book fairs. Learning how to communicate with people is the skill she values the most and it has taught her how to support artists, how to work with suppliers, how to ask for help, how to talk about money, and how to spot if someone is serious about a project or not.

Her studio, Colorama, combines various practices around book making, so Maierski perceives herself in a very multifaceted way – as a publisher, printer, art director, teacher, bookbinder and curator. When it comes to the content, the publications the studio produces are representations of new, progressive and experimental voices in comic books and serial narration. She sees publishing as an artistic, collaborative practice and as a democratic tool for participating in political and artistic discourses. 'I try to find ways to make book making and printing, and discourse about them, accessible. Making books, putting your voice into a printed matter is such a simple and affordable way of getting your position out there,' she says.

The Seminar, by Marie Weber.

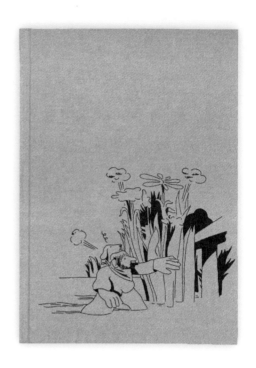

The Train, by Antoine Cossé.

Maierski is less concerned about the printing aspect of books, and is instead drawn to those who construct narratives in a unique way. She is more interested in how books are structured and put together than in the actual content. 'It can be about cars or about fairies; in the end I don't really care. I find it very fascinating how writers, book makers or artists find that peculiar balance of saying enough but not so much that they end up with something cliché or banal,' she explains.

Her favourite technique is RISO printing. When it comes to materials, she enjoys using both high- and low-quality ones in an object. Her taste has evolved through time – she likes book cloth as much as she likes paperclips. 'The eclectic is present in all my books. I really like that,' she says.

Her creative process mostly involves her sitting down with someone and talking through a random idea. Through talking, this idea will explode into a thousand new

Clubhouse#13,
with cover illustration by Aisha Franz.

Runaway Hearts, by Sean Christensen.

ones, and then she will write emails to everyone she wants to get involved, in order to realise it. When everyone is placed, she gets to work, which means adjusting the timeline and outlining what the main point of the project is. 'I think I would actually be a very good process engineer. I can wrap my head quite nicely around all the different things that need organising and taking care of to make a whole project work,' she says.

What Maierski enjoys most about her practice is gaining an insight into another person's work and supporting them to make it the best it can be at that moment. 'I enjoy it so much when artists are surprised by their own work or really feel they've dared something and succeeded. It is an incredible feeling to plan and make a book for a long time and then hold the first bound copy in your hands,' she says.

A Trick of the Light – Folds in Folds, by Jeong Hwa Min.

Palmeral, by Sara Perovic.

Making books, putting your voice into a printed matter is such a simple and affordable way of getting your position out there.

Asami Murakami

Asami Murakami (born in Tochigi, Japan) is a book designer and bookbinder. She spent her formative years growing up in the countryside of Tochigi – a prefecture north of Tokyo. Murakami moved to the UK to study in 2005, honing her skills in bookbinding with a BA in Book Arts at the London College of Communication. On returning to Japan, Murakami worked in a book design studio in Tokyo for four years, where she trained in the Japanese craft of book design. After that, she spent some time working as a freelance designer and bookbinder.

In August 2020 Murakami opened her first studio in Hamamatsu, Shizuoka Prefecture, Japan. Located on a street corner in a friendly, old-fashioned neighbourhood, the studio is open to locals to come and go as they please. The studio forms part of a multifunctional space in a renovated old Japanese house that is also home to a café, restaurant, event space, food market and co-working office.

Murakami avoids the term 'community' when describing her studio and the surrounding area: 'I feel I may be discriminating against people who think that they aren't a part of this community, so I deliberately avoid using the word "community". Instead, she prefers to keep her focus on the client–collaborator–artist relationship and on the book itself.

Covering everything from artists' books, special editions, family albums, notebooks and collaborative book projects to more conventional book designs, Murakami's practice is incredibly varied. One day she might be making a special edition by hand, and the next she might be designing a book for mass publication. Her work also extends to restoring old books and running bookbinding workshops around Japan.

The old guillotine was reinstalled on Murakami's working table. It used to be
in the atelier of Miyata Ranson, a folk crafts artist in Matsumoto Prefecture.

Observation Notebook was an original product of Murakami bindery. Made from disused kimonos, all different from each other.

Making things both by hand and using new technologies is important to Murakami, and she reflects that both methods have the potential to show her a book 'which hasn't been seen yet'. Her favourite moment as an artist and book maker comes, she says, from 'seeing the process by which a raft of words on a sheet becomes a book'.

Murakami takes a sustainable approach to book making: 'I don't make more books than are necessary. I don't stock more copies than necessary, and I don't use more materials than necessary. Restoring and repairing old books is an important part of my practice. I suppose that's how I play my part in the "ecosystem" of books.'

When it comes to her creative process, Murakami likes to listen to her books – the sound of the paper, thread, glue, and the voice of the book's content itself. She attempts to give a form to all of these qualities. 'I think the contents and appearance of a book should be treated equally,' she asserts.

Murakami deviates from the norm when it comes to her choice of materials, using cloth that is not widely used in bookbinding, like discarded kimonos, and she is drawn to the multifaceted nature of paper. The paper, in fact, is the aspect of books that most inspires her. 'The sound of paper when you read, the change in its colour and the feel of paper as time goes by;

ASAMI MURAKAMI

the way printed words distort when you turn the pages, and the smell of ink and paper,' she explains. She is influenced by the French poet Stéphane Mallarmé's *The Book,* and admires the work of Fumio Tachibana, a Japanese artist and graphic designer, whose work gives her a sense of joy.

Murakami believes that the wider revival in craft and the growing interest in the handmade are enriching contemporary culture, saying, 'It's good to give a form to your own thoughts by your hands. Once you make something by hand, you change the way you see it.'

Beautiful kimonos were found during renovation of the space; they are made of fine silk and other fabrics, all hardly worn.

Below: The bindery is located on a
street corner. People look in curiously
when they pass by and ask 'What are
you making?' Some people come in
and ask how to make a book.
Right: Murakami likes making books
while looking at the people who come
and go, and listening to the sounds
of the street.

I think the contents and appearance
of a book should be treated equally.

Book/Shop

Growing up in the Phoenix suburb of Scottsdale, Erik Heywood (born in Arizona, USA) longed for the green fields of England rather than the desert where he grew up, which, he recognises, a lot of people romanticise. 'I never could get very romantic about cactus and other plants that stab you if you get too close,' he says. After studying English at college and dropping out early to pursue a career of, as he puts it, 'loafing around in libraries and taking long walks', Heywood took a succession of design-related jobs in New York and California, including retail concept and interior design. 'I find retail in general a fascinating experiment in the quest to make art meet commerce,' he says.

Book/Shop began life as a website in 2011. 'It grew out of several blogs I'd been writing since 2007 about all kinds of things around books that weren't actually

the books themselves. Then I finally decided to start selling those things, with
books as well,' he recalls. After a year
and a half supporting the website with
occasional pop-ups in New York and San
Francisco, he opened his first physical
location in Oakland, California, in 2013.
In addition to Book/Shop, Heywood has
also worked as the co-creative director of
branding agency Partners & Spade, with
founder Andy Spade, since 2019.

Book/Shop sells rare and unusual books,
but Heywood does not, strictly speaking,
consider it a bookstore. 'It's a shop *about*
books, and about the reading experience.
We sell books, artwork related to books
and reading, reading accessories, furni-
ture for books, etc.,' he explains.

The project has never been just about
books themselves, but the world that
supports and surrounds books, from
bookshelf design, to reading chairs and
obscure poetic passages. 'I like to think
that early on I helped people see loving
books as a beautiful way of life. Much
of what I do still aims at that. I've never
had ambitions to make Book/Shop an
archetypical bookstore, as much as I love
them. I feel like there's room in the "book
ecosystem" for at least one store like
mine,' he says.

Heywood and his team are focused in their
selection and do not hunt online for books,
instead choosing to sell what they find
organically or what they discover through
other people. They predominantly sell

books pertaining to literature and the arts. All their books must be in near-perfect condition, regardless of their age. Of this process, Heywood elaborates: 'Books generally must have something charming about them to be included as well. That part is impossible to analyse. I can just *tell* if a book is right for us or not.'

The books that he admires are not necessarily unusually designed, but they do need to be well made. 'I like books that feel good in your hand, have a pleasing weight, lay flat when you open them, have paper that stays white and bright over many years, and that smell good as they age (it's said that some books smell good as they age because the decay of the glue and fibres in the paper create a compound chemically similar to vanilla). A fact I love,' he says.

Heywood regularly collaborates with people from a diverse range of fields, always with a link back to books. 'One thing I love about books is that everything is in books. Travel, fashion, poetry, gardening, jokes, art, everything. To me this gives booksellers the permission to get involved with everything,' he says.

On the future of bookselling, Heywood isn't concerned. Instead, he recognises that bookselling over the centuries has always offered up new challenges and is a labour of love. As he puts it, 'I believe that, as long as that kind of love continues, people will find a way to open bookshops that respond to their times. I don't worry much about the future of books themselves either. To me, it would be like worrying about the future of chocolate or sunny days at the park. They're too elemental, and pleasant, and satisfying to ever be really replaced. If there had never been books before and digital texts had come first and then somebody suddenly started making books, I think people would absolutely love them. And anyway, I see so many young people who grew up with everything digital, and they're opening bookshops, or starting presses, or crowding book fairs, and I don't really think bookshops will go away. Maybe they'll just evolve.'

One thing I love about books is that everything is in books... To me this gives booksellers the permission to get involved with everything.

Reading list

A suggested reading list from the library at the London Centre for Book Arts, a unique 400+ collection of books about books, printing, design, and related subjects. Some of the titles below have been referenced in this book by us or one of the contributors, while others represent a selection of books that have shaped the way we, as artists and makers, understand books today.

An Anthology of Decorated Papers
P.J.M. Marks
Thames & Hudson, 2015

Artists Books: A Critical Survey of the Literature
Stefan Klima
Granary Books, 1998

The Art of the Fold: How to Make Innovative Books and Paper Structures
Ulla Warchol, Hedi Kyle
Laurence King Publishing, 2018

The Art of Marbled Paper: Marbled Patterns and How to Make Them
Einen Miura
Zaehnsdorf, 1989

Book
James Langdon
Eastside Projects, 2010

The Book on Books on Artists Books
Arnaud Desjardin
The Everyday Press, 2011

Bookbinding: A Step by Step Guide
Kathy Abbott
The Crowood Press, 2010

Bookbinding: The Complete Guide to Folding, Sewing & Binding
Miriam Waszelewski, Franziska Morlok
Laurence King Publishing, 2018

Booktrek
Clive Phillpot
JRP | Ringier, 2012

The Century of Artists' Books
Johanna Drucker
Granary Books, 2004

Color Library: Research into Color Reproduction and Printing
David Keshavjee, Guy Meldem, Julien Tavelli (eds.)
JRP | Ringier, ECAL, 2018

The Coming of the Book: The Impact of Printing 1450–1800
Lucian Febvre, Henri-Jean Martin
Verso Books, 2010

Danish Artists' Books
Thomas Hvid Kromann, Louise Hold Sidenius, Maria Kjær Themsen, Marianne Vierø
Walther König, 2016

The Detroit Printing Co-op: the Politics of the Joy of Printing
Danielle Aubert
Inventory Press, 2019

Divine Art, Infernal Machine: The Reception of Printing in the West from First Impressions to the Sense of an Ending
Elizabeth Eisenstein
University of Pennsylvania Press, 2011

Five Hundred Years of Printing
S.H. Steinberg
Penguin, 1974

Form of the Book Book
Sara De Bondt, Fraser Muggeridge
Occasional Papers, 2009

The Gutenberg Galaxy: The Making of Typographic Man
Marshall McLuhan
University of Toronto Press, 1967

Japanese Bookbinding: Instructions from a Master Craftsman
Kojiro Ikegami
Weatherhill, 2012

Japanese Papermaking: Traditions, Tools and Techniques
Timothy Barrett
John Weatherhill, Inc., 1983

Kolkata: City of Print
Mara Züst
Spector Books, 2019

The Library Was
OOMK
Book Works, 2018

*Making Books: A Guide to Creating
Hand-crafted Books by the London
Centre for Book Arts*
Ira Yonemura, Simon Goode
Pavilion Books, 2017

*Natural Enemies of Books: A Messy History
of Women in Printing and Typography*
Maryam Fanni, Matilda Flodmark
and Sara Kaaman
Occasional Papers, 2020

NO-ISBN: On Self-publishing
Bernhard Cella, Leo Findeisen, Anges Blaha
Salon für Kunstbuch, 2015

*No Longer Innocent: Book Art
in America 1960–1980*
Betty Bright
Granary Books, 2005

*Papermaking: The History and
Technique of an Ancient Craft*
Dard Hunter
Dover Publications, 1978

A People on the Cover
Glenn Ligon
Ridinghouse, 2015

*Post-Digital Print: The Mutation
of Publishing since 1894*
Alessandro Ludovico
Onomatopee, 2012

*The Print Shop: A Celebration of Print
and 40 Years of Calverts*
Alice Pattullo
Design for Today, 2017

The Printing Press as an Agent of Change
Elizabeth Eisenstein
Cambridge University Press, 2013

*Printing 1770–1970: An Illustrated History
of its Development and Uses in England*
Michael Twyman
The British Library, Oak Knoll Press
and Reading University Press, 1998

Publishing as Artistic Practice
Annette Gilbert (ed.)
Sternberg Press, 2016

*Publishing in the Realm of Plant Fibers
and Electrons*
Temporary Services, Kione Kochi
Half Letter Press, 2014

*Publishing Manifestos: An International
Anthology from Artists and Writers*
Michalis Pichler (ed.)
The MIT Press, 2019

*Recto/Verso: Art Publishing
in Practice, New York*
Hauser and Wirth, 2018

Semina Culture: Wallace Berman and his Circle
Michael Duncan, Kristine McKenna
DAP, 2015

S v Z
Tauba Auerbach
D.A.P./SFMOMA, 2020

*Some Notes on Books and Printing:
A Guide for Authors, Publishers and Others*
Charles Jacobi, with Esther McManus
and Sam Whetton
Temporal Drag (A6BOOKS), 2018

*Towards a Self Sustaining Publishing Model:
A ten minute lesson / rant / manifesto*
Marc Fischer
Half Letter Press, 2021

What Problems Can Artist Publishers Solve?
Temporary Services, PrintRoom Rotterdam
Half Letter Press, 2018

Photographic credits

Awagami Factory: pp. 149–153

Barnard & Westwood: p. 128

Blythe Brett: pp. 102, 104–105

Book Works: pp. 70-75

Candor Arts: pp. 65, 67–69

Celia Rose: p. 114

Charles Benton: pp. 78–81

Christophe Urbain: p. 52

Deborah Suchman Zeolla: p. 77

Dunja Opalko: pp. 174, 176–181

Éditions du Livre: pp. 54–56

Edward Emberson: pp. 112–113, 115

Emilie Fayet: pp. 119–123

Evelyn Teploff-Mugii from living-form.com: p. 109

Florian Kleinefenn: p. 63

Gülsüm Güler: p. 201

Harlee Mollenkopf: pp. 212–217

Hendrik Altmeyer: p. 200

Hideaki Hamada: p. 106

Ira Yonemura: pp. 4–5, 7, 8, 9, 12, 222–223

Johanna Maierski: pp. 201–205

John Hammond: pp. 95, 156

Jonathan Frederick Turton: pp. 195–199

Julian Love: pp. 124, 127

Kristin Perers: pp. 99–100

Ko Kado: p. 107

Laurel Parker Book: pp. 25, 28-29

Louis Rogers: pp. 165, 162–163, 166

Louise Quigno : pp. 26–27

Mark Cropper : pp. 160–161, 164

Marina Denisova: pp. 110–111

Michèle Garrec: pp. 142–147

Natsuki Kuroda: p. 208

Neil Harrison: pp. 10 (left), 11, 92, 94, 154

Nicolas Waltefaugle: pp. 53, 57

Outer Space Press: pp. 31–35

Paavo Lehtonen: pp. 85, 87–89

Prudence Cuming Associates Ltd.: back cover, pp. 93, 96–97, 157, 159

Richard Sanderson & Esme Winter: pp. 116–117

Ringo Cheung: p. 61

Robin Silas Christian: p. 10 (right)

Sanchez Benton architects: p. 187

Stéphane Ouzonoff: pp. 139–141